January Joy

From gloomy to glorious,

kick-start your year in 10 simple steps!

Sophie Hayward

Copyright © 2024 Sophie Hayward

All rights reserved.

ISBN:9798332247279

The information provided in this book is for entertainment purposes only and should not replace professional medical advice. Consult with a healthcare provider before implementing any changes to your health regimen.

While all reasonable care has been taken during the preparation of this book, its recipes and instructions contained herein, the author cannot accept responsibility for any consequences arising from the use thereof or from the information contained therein.

DEDICATION

To my family, who bring me joy.

CONTENTS

Introduction	Pg 7
1 Organise	Pg 9
2 Cosify	Pg 18
3 Reflect	Pg 25
4 Resolve	Pg 30
5 Revitalise	Pg 37
6 Pamper	Pg 50
7 Develop	Pg 58
8 Explore	Pg 64
9 Connect	Pg 70
10 Celebrate	Pg 78
Daily Mood Boosts	Pg 97
Conclusion	Pg 129

INTRODUCTION

I once read in a magazine that January is like marmite - people either love it or hate it.

The words came back to me several years later at a New Year's Eve party following a particularly tipsy rendition of Auld Lang Syne. As the fireworks fizzled away and fellow revellers began their unsteady journey home, negative remarks drifted through the cold night air...

...'Don't want to go back to work', 'Roll on summer', 'Only another year until next Christmas!', 'I'm moving somewhere hot!' and 'Ugh, it's January already!'.

It suddenly occurred to me that although I had encountered many who happily declared an aversion to the first month of the year, I'd never met anyone who claimed to love it - or even like it!

As the days passed by, I found myself on a quest to find just one person who welcomed the arrival of January, but after listening to similar comments from family, friends, neighbours, my dentist and the postie, I had to face the fact - most people love...to hate it. It might have been my imagination but even my dog looked disappointed.

And who could blame them? After all the fuzzy and warm festive fun, January arrives with a thud of reality which leaves many in the cold.

As Big Ben chimes December goodbye, a Cinderella-esk phenomenon occurs. Decorations enthusiastically put up only weeks ago, lose their sparkle. Delicious treats once greeted with relish become an irritating reminder of tighter waistbands and scoffing chocolates for breakfast seems inappropriate. The bank account that was so full of promise lies depressingly empty and as for pay day - that may as well be in the misty dawn of a futuristic world.

Work looms on the horizon and dreary weather brings no cheer. Post festive farewells and reports that separations rank highest at this time of year contribute to a generally unsettled feeling. It's a wonder that anyone can drag themselves out of bed in the morning!

But not me. Apparently, I am one of those rare beings that love January!

Don't get me wrong, I'm not a gushy type and most of my friends would call me a realist, but I do love a fresh start and believe - as my dear Dad often used to say - that you have to make the best of life, which leads me to my next point.

January accounts for approximately ONE TWELFTH OF A LIFETIME! Quite an eye opener when expressed in those terms, so why do people waste so many of their precious hours yearning for it to be over? Like a blanket of fresh snow, January signifies a new chapter waiting to be written, which should be embraced.

So, here it is. My humble attempt to convert the haters to lovers - a mini resistance against the masses who wish it away. Read on to discover how adding a little fuel to the dying embers of New Year will give your January a beautiful glow!

N.B. The book consists of ten steps, which should be read in order. Each step offers ideas, advice, entertainment and activities to inspire you to make the very best of January - and beyond! Select those which are best suited to your needs, lifestyle and budget. I hope you enjoy the process and find your January Joy!

1. ORGANISE

After the activity and excesses of December, we should welcome January with open arms as a time to prepare for the year ahead. A constructive first step is to get rid of any clutter weighing us down. As well as enhancing our physical environment, research shows that a little organisation can be comforting, cathartic and a practical response to 'Janxiety'. It is also a great way to pass the time before payday!

Farewell Festivities ~ A good place to start is to pack away the festive decorations, but before you stuff them into boxes and push them aside for another year - take stock. Untangle lights and sort and gather anything that is broken or unwanted to discard, recycle or donate. Treat yourself to a few new ornaments in the January sales for a nice surprise when they re-emerge in December.

January Clean ~ Don't wait until spring to do the dirty work when you will feel more inclined to be outside - use the dull days of January instead! This can be as demanding as you desire, it's entirely up to your energy levels. You may feel like purging every wardrobe and chest of drawers in the house or simply get rid of a few things that aren't needed anymore, such as unwanted gifts.

You might focus on a room that would benefit from a thorough reconfiguration of storage space, or just clean out a kitchen cupboard or two. Whatever your approach, it will keep you active, provide a sense of achievement and you may even find a lost treasure.

You are also in good company as the process takes place all over the world by various cultures, using methods deeply rooted in tradition and ritual;

JANUARY JOY

Oosouji *translates to 'big cleaning' and is practised by the Japanese in preparation for New Year. The method symbolises the removal of impurities and negative energy in order to welcome good luck. It takes place at the end of the year and operates clockwise and top down through each room, with attention on removing stains (which may be a reminder of negativity from the past) and the immediate removal of rubbish and unwanted items.*

Khaneh-tekani *sees families prepare for Iranian New Year with a cleaning ritual which translates to 'shaking down the house'. It concentrates on items that don't tend to get cleaned regularly during the year, such as carpets, furniture, silverware, cupboards, paintwork, and windows. Many burn sandalwood to enhance air quality and buy new houseware to create a fresh atmosphere.*

Döstädning *is translated as Swedish death cleaning! This method places emphasis on decluttering the home and the mind through organising possessions to prevent families from being overburdened in the event of a loved one passing away. It involves sorting through personal items, such as clothes and photographs, gifting them gradually and thoughtfully to younger family members while keeping a box of personal memories. It encourages donating and recycling instead of stashing.*

Xiaonian *translates as preliminary eve when Chinese families give their home a spring clean in preparation for Lunar New Year celebrations. The traditional cleaning ritual is an important part of the preparations, believed to bring good fortune into the home by driving away any negative energy gathered over the year. The house is cleaned from top to bottom with cupboards and wardrobes given close attention. Broken items are repaired and some repaint doors and window frames in 'lucky' red - a colour associated in China with good fortune and life-generating energy.*

La Limpia *is a tradition performed in Mexico between Christmas and New Year. Homes are swept from back to front with a broom to cleanse the space from negativity. Dust is flung out of the front door symbolising 'out with the old and in with the new', before mopping, scrubbing and organising to welcome positivity in time for New Year.*

JANUARY JOY

Wardrobe Wonderful ~ Treat your clothes to a January makeover. It is so satisfying to get rid of any garments you don't wear well to create space for better ones. Sort clothes into piles to keep, donate, sell or recycle. If you haven't worn an everyday item for over a year, chances are you won't in the future - so let it go.

Colours that drain you, items that don't quite fit and pieces that make you feel less than your best should be set free. This may be difficult but be strong! If you really can't bear to part with truly sentimental items, (I still have my Levis 501s that I wore as a skinny student), vacuum pack them out of the way.

Now for the fun part. Identify any gaps in your remaining wardrobe and treat yourself to a few new pieces to give it a boost. If funds are low then host a clothes swap party with friends and neighbours, visit charity shops, (which are usually inundated after the festive season), or check out pre-loved apps where one person's trash can be another's treasure. I still can't believe my luck at finding a beautiful leather jacket for £5!

Blooming Brilliant ~ Harsh weather may be raging but if you are lucky enough to have an outdoor area to call your own, get cosy and browse through seed and bulb catalogues for a few hours. Channel phytophile Brontë from the film 'Green Card' as you plan your space to grow tasty produce and glorious flower displays to enjoy in the warmer days ahead.

Hardy plants such as apple, pear and plum trees, blueberries, blackberry and raspberry canes, rhubarb, bare root roses, lilies, pansies and cyclamen can all be planted outside in the colder months.

Other plants can be sown and left inside on a sunny windowsill or a greenhouse including aubergines, cauliflower, chillies, leeks, lettuce, onions, parsnips and strawberries as well as snapdragons, begonias, delphiniums, geraniums, petunias and sweet peas. Let your imagination run riot.

Trusty Transport ~ Breaking down at any time of the year is inconvenient and annoying but during the winter it can be particularly stressful. Organise a maintenance check on your bike or car (especially before long journeys) and consider an emergency roadside rescue policy if you don't have one.

Check tyres, lights, oil, fuel, wipers, brakes, batteries and antifreeze. Pack a basic survival kit in the boot which should include a thermal blanket, phone charger, water, calorie dense snacks, such as energy bars, spade, walking boots, coat, torch and an emergency reflective triangle in case you break down and need to abandon your vehicle. It may sound extreme but it is always best to be prepared.

Finance Effectively ~ Your financial position can have a direct impact on mental wellbeing, so don't hide from it - deal with it! Sleepless nights caused by anxiety about money can be alleviated when you identify areas where you can save. Take control by searching for better credit card deals and insurance costs. Reduce energy bills, review phone and broadband charges, cancel non-essential subscriptions and make a proper budget for food, leisure and extras and then stick to it.

Super Savvy ~ Explore ways to make better life choices. Instead of eating out, spend quality time in the kitchen honing your culinary skills. Don't travel to work alone, get to know a colleague better during a car share. Swap coffee shop visits for delicious home brews in a brand-new coffee flask and say goodbye to unhealthy processed food with super nutritious packed lunches - your colleagues will wish they had done the same!

Find fun alternatives to expensive leisure activities. Forget the cinema, start a film club with friends. Boost your body with a healthy hike instead of shopping for things you don't need. Organise a staycation with your besties rather than booking an expensive weekend away - in my experience these can be a blast!

Sort Digital Space ~ Work is demanding enough without a desktop full of junk to hinder your progress, so take some time to delete any unused apps, clear out old downloads and remove unnecessary files. Create a proper filing system for your digital documents and stay safe online by changing passwords and checking antivirus and security software is up to date.

Take Charge of Time ~ Reflect on your daily routine. Is it supportive to your schedule or are there improvements that can be made? Getting up a little earlier, doing some preparation the evening before or delegating tasks instead of doing everything yourself can really enhance your day. Manage your year ahead by updating your new calendar with important appointments, birthdays, etc. Avoid becoming overwhelmed by making a daily to do list and reduce brain burden by creating weekly meal planners, which can be rotated to suit you.

Declutter in Seven Steps

1. *Choose a room in your home which you feel would benefit from a good sort out.*

2. *Decide which storage units within the room you need to focus on and in what order, e.g. wardrobe then chest of drawers and bookshelves.*

3. *Allocate an approximate amount of time to sort through each unit and stick to it. You may have the motivation to complete it in a day or want to take it easier and complete one unit per week.*

4. *Make space for keep, donate, sell and recycle piles.*

5. *Work through the units efficiently, placing items into the relevant pile. Do not get distracted by anything you rediscover - you can do that later!*

6. *Place the sell pile to one side to tackle another day, then transport donations and recycling to the appropriate places before you change your mind!*

7. *Organise your remaining items back into their relevant storage units. Utilise areas you may not have considered before, such as underneath beds or on top of wardrobes. Use attractive boxes and baskets to help make your room even more spacious and appealing.*

Hug in a Mug – Gingerbread Latte

January is a perfect time to indulge in delectable hot drinks which warm and soothe like a comforting hug. Here are a few of my favourite recipes which add joy to my day.

This mouthwatering gingerbread latte is a combination of fragrant spices and flavours which will warm you up in no time.

Serves 2. You will need:

Espresso or strong coffee

1 pinch each of ground cinnamon, ginger, cloves and nutmeg.

1 tbsp each of molasses and syrup

2 drops of vanilla extract

Milk of your choice – plant or dairy based

Method:

Heat up the coffee in a pan – enough for two mugs. Add the spices, syrup, vanilla and molasses, then whisk and bring to a simmer. Froth the milk until foamy, then pour the coffee mixture into the mugs and top with the frothy milk. Add a squirt of whipped cream if desired. Enjoy!

DID YOU KNOW... that in 45 BC, New Year's Day was celebrated on January 1st for the very first time?

Not long after becoming Roman dictator, Julius Caesar decided the traditional Roman Calendar needed reform and designed a new one. It followed the solar year instead of the lunar cycles and was known as the Julian calendar.

The original calendar had only ten named months of March to December as the winter period was considered dormant in terms of agriculture and a time of peace, not war.

The new calendar year added the months of January and February and the beginning of the year began on January 1st.

January Entertainment

Read:

Never Die in January by Alan Scholefield (1993)

Play:

January Stars ~ Sting (1993)

You in January ~ The Wonder Years (2015)

Watch:

January 2nd (2006)

A New Year party in the country for a reunion of London city dwellers may be too late for resolutions, but not for revenge.

2. COSIFY

January may leave some feeling blue but just because the weather is dreary doesn't mean our surroundings have to be. It is what we do with our living space that makes it inviting, so when the decorations have been taken down and the calendar lies refreshingly empty, take time to cosify the home.

Lighten Up ~ Lighting can have a significant effect on any room as well as a considerable impact on mental wellbeing. Since winter means less daylight hours, it is a good idea to let in as much natural light as possible and encourage it to 'bounce around'. Illuminate your home with bright white walls, reflective surfaces, such as large well-placed mirrors and clean, uncluttered windows.

Place Your Space ~ The feeling of spaciousness as a result of taking down festive decorations always pleasantly surprises me. January means more time gazing inwards at the fire than outwards through the window, so position your furniture to make the most of what the month has to offer. A little rearranging can be a simple but effective way to enhance your living area and add a welcome sense of novelty for the winter days.

Embrace Colour and Texture ~ Discover a new appreciation for January by injecting your home with a variety of cheerful soft furnishings to suit your budget. Comforting textures ease the senses by inviting touch, drawing you into the present and splashes of colour can really energise a room. Nestle into vibrant throws and cushions and treat your feet with a deep pile rug in rich hues.

Make bedtime inviting by using brushed cotton sheets, a squashy duvet and thick knitted blankets in calming tones and enhance a long soak in the tub with fresh, fluffy towels in the bathroom. Display the organic beauty of indoor flowers which bloom through the winter, such as a Poinsettia - known for its striking red petals.

Glow in the Dark ~ Ditch harsh fluorescent ceiling glare for intimate pools of light. Candles create a calming atmosphere and keep you focused on the present. Table lamps and standing lamps bring depth and add a soothing effect as they bathe rooms in a gentle radiance.

Create an ambient glow by draping fairy lights over plants and along window sills or place them in large glass vases to twinkle in dark corners. In my opinion, January would not be the same without them!

Get Fired Up ~ The sight and sound of a crackling fire is hard to beat and instantly emanates warm rustic vibes. If you are lucky enough to have a fireplace, ensure the chimney has been swept then grab some logs and make the effort to use it.

Alternatively, safely place large candles in the grate which look beautiful when lit. If you haven't got a fireplace there are electric alternatives which offer fabulous faux flames. If you don't have the room, play a free fire stock video on your digital screen - mesmerising when you need some extra comfort and cheer.

Cosy To Go ~ Want to snuggle up in a blanket but have things to do? Keep toasty warm by wearing thick socks, soft woollen sweaters and fleecy leggings or a fluffy onesie with slipper boots. This is an ideal way to feel snug wherever you are in the house and so comfy to change into when you return home on a cold day.

Make Scents ~ Aromas work wonders to lift spirits and relax the senses. Whether you prefer fruity, fresh, floral or spicy fragrances, use aromatherapy burners, diffusers and automatic air fresheners to infuse your home with wonderful scents.

Try relaxing lavender in the living room and citrus for a lift in the kitchen and bathroom. Always use according to instructions.

Bring the Outside In ~ Just because it's grey outside doesn't mean you should miss out on lush greenery. Research shows that plants in the home help to produce a calming mental effect and improve air quality - important when you spend a lot of time indoors. Place them around the home to soothe your mind and enhance productivity and positivity.

Display Your Faves ~ Personalise space and surround yourself with happy memories by displaying treasured items all around you. It could be an ornament you have bought, something you have created or a cherished photograph, such as a sunny holiday snap, to remind you of warmer days ahead. Frame and hang it to produce a visual effect which will boost your mood whenever you see it. Place a few together for extra impact.

Cosify your Bedroom

Your bedroom is a place to relax and recharge, so transform it into a peaceful sanctuary.

Clean and declutter the room to create balance and harmony and arrange bedroom furniture to allow space for ease of movement.

Encourage tranquillity by minimising electronics and sensory overload.

Choose a restful colour scheme and accessorise with soft fabrics and textures.

Upscale your bed by adding brushed cotton sheets, an extra-large duvet, fluffy blankets and plenty of plump pillows and squashy cushions.

Indulge your toes with a little luxury by adding a deep pile rug beside your bed.

Bedeck bedroom walls with framed photos and pieces of art that are joyful to wake up to and comforting to drift off to.

Make your bedside table a haven of good books - include a gratitude journal and a jar of calming lavender sprigs.

Bring the outside in and purify the air by adding a potted plant, such as a Peace lily, to your bedroom.

Add fairy lights and bedside lamps for a comforting glow and create a soft ambience by using warm LED lightbulbs.

Invest in comfy pyjamas that allow you to curl up and relax without restriction. For extra warmth, think fluffy socks and snug fleece layers.

Hug in a Mug – Mulled Cider

If you drink the same hot beverages every winter, January could be the perfect time to mix things up a little. Mulled cider infused with warm spices is guaranteed to lift spirits on a dull January afternoon. Use cloudy apple juice for a non-alcoholic version.

Serves 6. You will need:

1 litre of cloudy cider and ½ litre of ginger beer

1 orange and 1 apple

10 cloves and 1 star anise

A few cinnamon sticks

1 tbsp of honey

Method:

Pour the cider and ginger beer into a large saucepan. Add the cinnamon sticks, star anise and honey and bring to the boil. Press the cloves into the orange skin and add to the pan then simmer for five minutes. Pour into mugs with a slice of apple and segment of cooked orange. Enjoy!

DID YOU KNOW... that January was named after the Roman god, Janus?

Janus was the spirit of doorways, gates and archways – a protector of transitions who symbolised endings and beginnings.

He was represented as a literal two-faced head, one facing backward in reflection and resolution and the other looking forward to the coming year, with the ability to see the future.

Janus was worshipped at the commencement of many significant occasions, including harvesting and the start of the military season in March.

Temples were built for him and a festival in his honour took place in January. The Romans would offer Janus sacrifices and promise good conduct for the year ahead.

January Entertainment

Read:

The Ten Thousand Doors of January by Alix E. Harrow (2019)

Play:

January Hymn ~ The Decemberists (2011)

January ~ Disclosure (2013)

Watch:

January (2018)

A former superhero finds himself in a world where he has no power.

3. REFLECT

Nature offers guidance on how we should be spending our time and January is perfect for connecting with its vibe. The winter solstice may have come and gone but chilly days are still ahead of us. Take notice of what's happening outside - the lack of activity suggests this is not a period to throw ourselves into major projects and drain reserves. Instead, we should lean into January with a sigh of relief, reflect on the past year and consider the one ahead.

The act of reflection is a perfect starting point when laying intentions for the coming year. Taking a break to contemplate and plan for the future is especially useful if you are feeling low as it may clarify any underlying concerns. Now is the time to deal with them, form a clear picture of who you are and where you want to be heading.

- Choose a quiet, comfortable space to relax with a notepad and clear your mind of distracting thoughts.

- Think about your life over the past year. Analyse what it has meant for you in terms of your partner, family, friends, work, leisure and health. How does it make you feel and why? What would you like to change? Are there any undesirable factors that keep recurring or enjoyable experiences you would like to repeat? Write them down.

- Think about you. Analyse what you believe you have accomplished in the past year. How does it make you feel and why? What would you like to change in order to feel more fulfilled and energised? What are your values and strengths and how would you like to be remembered? Write them down

    Don't mistake fulfilment with improvement. It's useful to know your weaknesses but better to focus on your strengths and enrich your future by achieving your potential.

- Finally, take some time to think about the good things you have in your life right now. Gather together your precious picture memories from the past year into an album (digital or hardcopy) and take time to reminisce.

Cherished photos and videos have the power to transport the mind back to enjoyable moments and provide an endorphin rush, which can boost wellbeing. The year has passed and this is a great way to acknowledge it. Take inspiration from the poem about the Roman god, Janus - composed by John Wadsworth Longfellow.

January

Janus am I; oldest of potentates;

Forward I look, and backward, and below

I count, as god of avenues and gates,

The years that through my portals come and go.

I block the roads, and drift the fields with snow;

I chase the wild-fowl from the frozen fen;

My frosts congeal the rivers in their flow,

My fires light up the hearths and hearts of men.

Longfellow, Henry Wadsworth, "The Poet's Calendar", Maine Historical Society, 2024

Hug in a Mug - Hot Chocolate

Indulge yourself with a cup of homemade velvety smooth hot chocolate with whipped cream and mini marshmallows - delicious on a cold January day. Be extra indulgent by adding peppermint or toffee sauce or a splash of brandy or rum!

Serves 1. You will need:

250 mls milk - dairy or plant based

1 tbsp of cocoa

2 tbsps of brown sugar

25g of dark chocolate

1 tbsp of whipped cream and a handful of mini marshmallows

Method:

Pour the milk into a pan, add the chocolate and heat until it melts. Whisk in the sugar and cocoa. Pour into a mug and add the cream and mini marshmallows on top. Enjoy!

DID YOU KNOW... that January is the time when Earth reaches Perihelion?

Earth rotates around the sun in an oval shape – an ellipse – which means it is regularly moving closer and further from the sun during the year. Perihelion is the time in Earth's orbit when it is closest to the sun and moving at its fastest. Although it does not directly affect Earth's temperature, the sun appears the largest in the sky on this day.

The term Perihelion was created by Johannes Kepler in 1596. It comes from Greek meaning around (peri) the sun (helios).

Perihelion day is gradually shifting forward over time. In 1246 it took place on December 21st (the winter solstice) but the day now occurs around January 4th.

January Entertainment

Read:

Doctor January by Rhoda Baxter (2014)

Play:

January Friend ~ The Goo Dolls (1998)

January Sunrise ~ Kevin Kendle (2007)

Watch:

New Year (2021)

A group of friends come together for a distressing New Year's Eve celebration, full of love and lies.

4. RESOLVE

Belief in the future encourages us to live life to the full and January arrives full of hope as New Year resolutions are planned with enthusiasm. Unfortunately, it appears to fall short on will power as these firm intentions are usually abandoned only weeks later. This is surprising since we have had four thousand years of practise - give or take!

According to history, resolutions have been evident throughout the ages, all the way back to the ancient Babylonians of 2000 BC. Their New Year occurred in spring and was celebrated with a religious festival called Akitu, where favour was sought with their gods by settling debts - including the return of borrowed equipment. The Babylonians believed that failure to keep their promise would result in their god's disapproval.

The ancient Romans assumed Babylonian traditions but it was the revolutionary Julius Caesar who altered the calendar and established January 1st as the start of the year, which took effect in 45 BC. The new month was named after their god, Janus, and the Romans would offer Janus sacrifices and promise good conduct for the year ahead.

During the Middle Ages, medieval knights would demonstrate knightly principles by taking the Vow of the Peacock at the end of the year, placing their hands upon a peacock, as the glorious colour of the plumage was thought to equal the king's majesty. In the 18th century, the founder of methodism, John Wesley, established a spiritual alternative to rowdy New Year merriments known as the Covenant Renewal. This included a form of resolution to renew a commitment to God.

The term 'New Year Resolution' is believed to have appeared for the first time in print during 1813 in a Boston newspaper, in reference to committing to better behaviour. The early 1900s observed a strict religious focus on resisting temptation but today's resolutions are usually a more secular affair with the emphasis on self-improvement.

Whatever the reason, time has revealed that we like the idea of improving the self. Unfortunately, studies show that many resolutions are ditched for being too unrealistic, vague or boring. As Mark Twain wrote:

'New Year's Day...now is the accepted time to make your regular annual good resolutions. Next week you can begin paving hell with them as usual.'

To ensure you get the year on the right track, forget the resolution frenzy and instead focus on **resolve**, defined as *'finding a solution to a problem or deciding firmly on a course of action'*, whereas the definition of resolution is *'a decision to do or not do something'*. This subtle but significant difference is the key to success as resolve brings depth to a decision-making process - which creates self-awareness, resilience and fulfilment.

Be C.L.E.A.R!

Clarify areas that you feel need attention in your life - use the notes from your reflection exercise.

List specific issues which you think are most important to address.

Envisage a distinct and realistic picture of what you want to achieve regarding these specific issues, then reinforce your ideas by writing them down.

Assemble your plan of action. With these end goals in mind, identify and allocate objectives to each month of the year, framing them positively. January is just the first step and achieving monthly targets will provide a sense of accomplishment - see page 33.

Review your objectives. Do they excite you and make you feel determined? If not, rethink them.

Tips for Success!

No one is able to control the future but we can certainly influence it. Learn from the past, seize the present and begin the year on a positive note.

- Gain support from those you trust by letting them know what you are aiming to achieve and ask for a little encouragement.

- Consider any weaknesses or commitments which may hinder your progress and how you can address them.

- Take it one day at a time, just keep moving forward and don't overthink it. Motivate yourself with rewards as you progress, such as a massage, a nice meal or a glass of wine - whatever suits your budget.

- If you don't hit your target, take a break, remind yourself of the progress already made and promise yourself that tomorrow will be a better day. Don't dwell on it, adapt - it is part of the process.

- Maintain a level of flexibility for the unforeseen. Rigid schedules can become a pressure you don't need, so allow yourself a little 'wriggle room'!

- Give form to your goals by setting your intentions on a vision board. Studies show that visualising your aims leads to a greater self-belief that you will succeed. Arrange inspirational images, words and colours which you feel best represent your ideas on a board, then place it somewhere you will regularly see it.

Example

January - 'Using reflection notes, I realise that although I enjoy my job, I don't feel that I am progressing in my current role. Achieving promotion within the next few years would increase self-worth, provide a new challenge, boost salary and improve long term prospects.'

February - organise certificates, update current CV and create an online portfolio, listing job related skills.

March - schedule regular periods of time to read about the latest industry developments and the opportunities it has to offer.

April - understand specifically what is wanted in terms of new responsibility and what is needed regarding skill advancement.

May - arrange a meeting with superior to discuss current performance and future opportunities and request relevant support.

June - utilise company resources to expand skill set and increase professional connections through social media platforms, workshops and networking events.

July - take a break.

August/September/October/November - focus on advised goals and professional development.

December - arrange a follow up meeting with superior to discuss progression and challenges in achieving your end goal. If you don't reach your goal on time, your organisation, networking and skill advancement will provide a firm base to further progress your career path.

JANUARY JOY

Hug in a Mug – Hot Buttered Rum

One of my simple pleasures is to curl up by the fire with a mug of something special and take time to savour each sip. Hot buttered rum is a mouthwatering treat which will warm you up on a chilly January evening.

Serves 2. You will need:

1 tbsp of brown sugar

2 tbsps of unsalted butter, melted

100 mls of dark rum

1 tsp of ground cinnamon and 2 cinnamon sticks

½ tsp of ground nutmeg

Method:

Add the sugar, ground cinnamon and nutmeg to a small bowl and mix. Gradually stir in the rum and melted butter. Divide the mixture between two mugs and top up with boiling water. Stir and add a cinnamon stick. Enjoy!

DID YOU KNOW... that January is commonly host to the Quadrantids meteor shower?

The Quadrantids meteor shower is one of the year's strongest and most consistent showers which appears in early January. At its peak it can produce up to twenty-five meteors per hour.

The meteors radiate from the constellation Bootes which is close to the Big Dipper although they get their name from the former constellation, Quadrans Muralis.

The meteors consist of asteroid fragments and comet debris. They emit a blue light as they vaporise in the Earth's atmosphere but are only visible for a few hours.

The best conditions to see the vibrant display is on a clear night sky with little light pollution, in the northern hemisphere. Make sure you take lots of warm layers, a hot drink and plenty of patience!

January Entertainment

Read:

A January Chill by Rachel Lee (2001)

Play:

January Rain ~ David Gray (2000)

January Rain ~ Shaw Horton (2023)

Watch:

Captain January (1936)

Relatives come to the rescue when a truancy officer separates a young girl from the lighthouse keeper who saved her life.

5. REVITALISE

We may feel sluggish and lack enthusiasm after the festivities but instead of crawling back under the duvet, January is a perfect time to focus on health. Before eye-rolling and tossing this book behind the sofa - relax - this isn't about high impact workouts or harsh diet regimes. This IS about beneficial changes within personal comfort zones to revitalise.

Restore!

After weeks of eating, drinking, partying, sofa surfing and falling into bed at all hours, it is unlikely you will greet January feeling your absolute best self. Take the opportunity to restore your former glory and get glowing!

Seize the Daylight ~ January days are short on natural light and you may have a strong urge to channel your inner bear and hunker down in the warmth, but getting out in the cold light of day can be good for you in many ways.

Exposure to sunlight releases endorphins and helps to regulate bodily rhythms of mood, sleep and appetite, as well as topping up vitamin D levels - crucial in supporting healthy bones, muscles and the immune system. Wrap up warm and get out as frequently as you can, even if it is just for ten minutes at a time.

If it is tricky to spend time outdoors, try using a light box which replicates natural outdoor light for a mood boosting effect. Place it where you spend the most time indoors - working or relaxing.

Structure Your Day ~ After the chaos of 'Twixtmas' when the days can seem to blend into each other, the certainty of a daily routine encourages focus, healthy habits and productivity. Walking my dog, followed by a shower and healthy breakfast, sets me up for the day.

Sweet Dreams ~ Even though we choose to ignore it on a fabulous night out or when binging box sets, most of us know that regular sleep is vital to help us throw back the bedcovers when the alarm goes off. This can be especially challenging in January, so end the day with a familiar routine to soothe body and mind in preparation for a peaceful night's sleep.

Lose the Snooze ~ January dawn rises later and with less natural light hitting your optic nerve, the production of the 'sleepy' hormone - melatonin - increases. We may feel like we need more sleep but guidelines suggest most adults need between six and nine hours a night, whatever time of the year.

Hormone production, body temperature and metabolism are affected by our circadian rhythm or 'body clock'. If it becomes irregular, it may lead to tiredness and irritability during the day. Be strong and avoid hitting that snooze button.

Movement, light and routine help the brain and body to wake up. Place your alarm clock out of reach so you have to physically get out of bed to switch it off and use an illuminating alarm lamp which gradually increases its brightness until it is time to get up. Set your alarm for the same time every morning, even at the weekend, as this consistency schedules the brain to wake at a specific time every day.

These habits support quality sleep with the added bonus that you get more time to do the things you like - in or out of bed!

A Beneficial Bedtime Routine

Stop eating a few hours before bedtime - this enables the body to heal overnight instead of having to digest food in your stomach.

Turn off technology an hour before bedtime to let your brain wind down.

Ensure an organised start to the next day by taking time to tidy the bedroom and prepare tomorrow's clothes.

Set the alarm clock and programme heating so the room is warm to wake up to.

Check the bedroom is not too hot or cold which can cause restlessness.

Let your worries float away as you sink into a warm scented bath - lavender is my favourite. Sipping chamomile herbal tea can also help you unwind.

Snuggle into a cosy bed - a squashy duvet, soft sheets and plump pillows all help.

Keep a pad and pencil by your bed to write down anything which may be troubling you as this allows your brain to relax and promotes a settled sleep.

Encourage upbeat closure on the day by feeling grateful for it - this helps bring any positive and uplifting events to the forefront of your mind.

Lack of movement helps the body to prepare for sleep, so lie back with a good book (read it or listen to an audible version) and feel yourself begin to drift.

Sweet dreams!

Energise!

Resolutions to 'get fit' in the New Year seem a little clichéd and I've lost count of the number of friends who join a gym yet hardly ever go! However, starting some regular exercise is one of the best things you can do to improve your physical and mental wellbeing. It releases endorphins to reduce stress, boosts immunity, supports fitness and makes you look and feel better.

Find Your Fit ~ Consult your healthcare provider before creating an enjoyable exercise routine to suit you and your lifestyle. The body produces chemicals based on emotion and dreading exercise will make it feel hard going, so choose something fun. It could be as simple as a lunchtime walk or some gentle yoga before bedtime. If you fancy something a little more challenging try weight training, running or dancing - mix it up a little!

No Excuses ~ There is always an opportunity to fit in some exercise. It could be walking the kids to school, cycling to work, taking the stairs instead of the lift, doing a set of lunges while waiting for the kettle to boil or star jumps during advert breaks. Commit to small goals and make sure you treat yourself as you reach them.

Fit Bits ~ Achieving the fitness level you desire will take time and being incentivised will help prevent demotivation. The trick to achieving consistency is to get your exercise in enjoyable chunks. Build up gradually to avoid injury or become disillusioned - there is no point running until you want to vomit!

Rather than doing one long session, break it up into a few mini sessions spread throughout the day. This can be more convenient and gentle approach and less overwhelming!

Exercise Outdoors ~ 'Brrrrr!' is usually the standard reaction when looking out of the window during January and being outside probably isn't top of your agenda. However, physical exercise in the fresh air is invigorating and burns more calories as your body has to work harder to regulate your core temperature. Dressing in layers and embracing the outdoors helps you get some of that important daily dose of vitamin D, connects you with nature and is an opportunity to meet other like-minded people.

Don't sit there shivering at the thought of it - just do it! Watch your breath evaporate while walking a nature trail or running through the park. If it snows, get your blood pumping and relive your youth by making a snowman, go sledging or enjoy a hike through a winter wonderland! Returning home to the warmth with endorphins flooding your system feels fantastic.

Exercise Light ~ January mornings and evenings are cold and dark so it's no wonder that many feel these times are unsuitable to exercise outside. Driving to an exercise class on black ice or going for a run in the dark is not safe, so it's worth planning what exercise you can do late morning or early afternoon, whether at work or home. Try a lunchtime exercise class - it is great for a physical and mental boost to avoid that 3pm slump!

Exercise at Home ~ Exercising in the comfort of your own home offers many benefits. It is private, cheap, convenient and can fit in around work and family. There are so many on-line options ranging from belly dancing to boxing, so choose a selection to keep it interesting. Don't forget that doing activities such as cleaning and gardening also contribute to fitness - if your body is moving, it's all good.

Nourish!

The type of food we eat can have a significant impact on how we feel - both physically and mentally. After the festive season, when the junk food hook is high, it may be tempting to keep reaching for more starchy, salty and sugary treats to achieve an instant fix. The cold weather also stimulates a yearning to eat for warmth and comfort, which doesn't help!

These cravings may be difficult to break, so don't - just make healthier choices. Now is the time to nourish your body to get you fighting fit for the year ahead. In my opinion, January is not the time to start a restrictive diet - save the salads and smoothies for when the days get warmer and lighter. Instead, think hearty winter warmers full of wholesome and seasonal ingredients to keep you feeling satisfied during the chilly weather, without piling on the pounds.

Set aside time during long winter evenings and bad weather weekends for some home cooking. Gain satisfaction from trying out new dishes, choosing fresh ingredients and bringing loved ones together to taste your creations. Whether you want to perfect your chilli or bake the ultimate healthy comfort snack, there are plenty of mouthwatering recipes available to try online.

Fruit and Vegetables ~ It is important to include plenty of these in your daily diet. They contain vitamins, minerals and phytochemicals and are packed with antioxidants, which decrease inflammation in the body. They are also a source of feel-good polyphenols and fibre which satisfy your gut.

Aim to eat a variety to maximise nutrient intake and boost your microbiome. Keep costs low and be eco-friendly by using seasonal produce, such as potatoes, carrots, cauliflower, onions, cabbage, leeks, sprouts, beetroot, parsnips, squash, swedes, apples, pears and rhubarb.

JANUARY JOY

Casseroles, Stews and Soups ~ Whether a consumer of meat and fish or a vegetarian or vegan, casseroles, stews and soups are a versatile way to consume many vegetables and are easy to make. Cook up a big batch to portion and freeze, to heat up for a quick restorative meal after a long day. Consider investing in a slow cooker to produce delicious creations while you get on with other things.

Stewpendous! ~ Fruit can be more palatable and easier to digest when it is cooked. Stewed apples and rhubarb are really tasty in a crumble served with a little custard. Poached pears and plums are delicious with a sprinkling of cinnamon and a drizzle of cream.

Veganuary ~ This annual campaign encourages people to try a plant-based diet for a month which studies have suggested is beneficial for the planet. Give it a try or dip your toe in by adding a vegan option to your weekly menu.

Wholegrain Fibre ~ Wholegrain fibre supports your digestive and immune system and helps keep you satisfied. Fibre rich foods include wholewheat pasta and brown rice, wholegrain bread and cereals, jacket potatoes, oats, seeds, pulses and beans. When you're feeling a bit peckish, wholegrain snacks are a healthy choice and keep you fuller for longer.

Oats ~ This wholegrain is a great source of complex carbohydrates and fibre which help you feel full and can balance blood sugar levels to enhance mood and prevent fatigue. Oats can be enjoyed in many forms, such as granola or porridge for breakfast to boost energy levels for the day ahead, or flapjacks and crumbles for a satisfying snack or pudding.

Legumes ~ As well as being filling, beans, lentils and chickpeas are a great source of zinc, magnesium, iron, selenium and B vitamins, which play an important role in regulating mood. Add them to soups, casseroles, wraps - whatever you fancy.

Nuts and Seeds ~ Providing you are not allergic, nuts and seeds are a great source of plant-based protein and healthy fats which are anti-inflammatory, as well as high in B vitamins, magnesium, zinc and selenium. They are tasty as a snack during the day but are calorie dense so eat in small amounts.

Fermented Foods ~ Fermented foods are high in probiotics which are believed to support the immune system. Try live yoghurt, kefir, kombucha, miso, sauerkraut, tempeh and pickled vegetables, such as kimchi, to improve gut health and boost mood.

Spices ~ Many spices add an extra kick to winter dishes and can also benefit health. Aromatic ginger and turmeric are tasty additions which are believed to have antimicrobial, antioxidant and immunity boosting properties. They are delicious added to soups, stews, rice and chickpeas.

Nutmeg and cinnamon are warming spices which contain compounds that are thought to lower blood pressure, improve mood, boost metabolism and reduce inflammation - add to hot drinks and porridge.

Omega-3 Fatty Acids ~ These are a group of essential fats that the body cannot produce itself so must be obtained through diet. Foods high in omega-3s include mackerel, salmon, sardines, tuna, chia seeds and soybeans. Research shows that regularly consuming omega-3s may help to reduce the likelihood of low mood as well as many other benefits for the body. Try to include oily fish in your diet a couple of times a week or take a high-quality supplement.

Vitamin D ~ Lack of vitamin D production in the body can lead to fatigue, joint pain and low mood. Get your daily dose of the sunshine vitamin by eating fatty fish (mackerel and salmon), portobello mushrooms, egg yolks and cheese or foods fortified with vitamin D including cereal, orange juice and soy milk.

Dark Chocolate ~ The taste, aroma and texture of chocolate can transport you. This delicious treat is believed to release a range of mood boosting compounds and health promoting flavonoids. Choose a quality chocolate with a high cocoa percentage to avoid too much fat and sugar.

Bananas ~ As well as being portable, tasty and full of nutrients, such as potassium, bananas are a great source of fibre. The fruit sugar in a banana, when eaten with the fibre, is released more slowly into the bloodstream which stabilises blood sugar levels and mood. Bananas are also high in vitamin B6 and tryptophan (especially those with green peel), and are a good source of prebiotics which help support gut health.

Honey ~ The taste is reason enough to eat this natural product but it also provides amazing benefits for the body. Discovered thousands of years ago, honey has been widely used for its therapeutic effects. It can help to boost energy, support gastric issues due to its antioxidant and anti-microbial properties, as well as being a natural antiseptic. Eat it on wholegrain toast and natural yoghurt or use it as a facemask!

Olive Oil ~ Many experts agree that this kind of fat is good for you as it is high in mono-unsaturated fat, contains antioxidants, has antibacterial and anti-inflammatory properties and protects against various ailments. It may also benefit your heart, brain, joints and more. Use as a dressing for salads and vegetables, add to soups, drizzle over bread and cook with it. Source a top-quality extra virgin olive oil for optimum health benefits.

Water ~ Central heating and cold weather can dry the atmosphere so ensure you stay hydrated to protect body and brain function. General guidelines suggest drinking six to eight glasses of water a day during the winter. Replace addictive caffeine and sugar with cleansing herbal teas, such as lemon, ginger, chamomile or fruit teas.

Alcohol ~ This also dehydrates. Alcohol tends to provide a social boost and aid relaxation but too much of it can be destructive to both mental and physical health. Reducing alcohol intake after the festivities may help increase energy levels, improve sleep quality and boost wellbeing.

Dry January ~ This campaign encourages people to live completely alcohol free for one month, to reap the health benefits and research other techniques which contribute to relaxation. Enjoy sampling the latest zero alcohol beers, wines and spirits and have fun discovering your favourite mocktail.

Be Selective ~ Finally, reducing junk in your diet shouldn't just be limited to what goes into your body - it's also about what you allow into your mind. Choose wisely who you spend time with, what you watch, read and listen to. It has an effect, so consume positive!

Hug in a Mug - Mexican Hot Chocolate

If you fancy something comforting but don't have a sweet tooth, try a mug of delicious Mexican hot chocolate. This recipe is spicy and rich but only slightly sweet - alter amount of sugar to taste.

Serves 2. You will need:

2 mugs of milk

3 tsps of unsweetened cocoa powder

2 tbsps of sugar

½ tsp of ground cinnamon and ¼ tsp of vanilla extract

A pinch of chilli powder and cayenne pepper

1 oz of bittersweet chocolate

Method:

Add the milk, cocoa powder, sugar, cinnamon, vanilla, chilli and cayenne to a saucepan. Whisk together and heat, add the chocolate and stir until it has melted and the mixture is hot. Divide between two mugs. Enjoy!

DID YOU KNOW... that the full moon in January is called Wolf Moon?

During ancient times it was usual to track the seasons by following the lunar month instead of the solar year, as we do now.

Ancient names for the full moon are thought to have come from Anglo Saxon, Germanic, and Native American origins and are still used today.

Anglo Saxons named January 'Wulfmonath', which is believed to have stemmed from times when hungry wolves would venture closer to humans, scavenging for food during the early part of the year.

Wolves generally become more active at night and howl in the direction of the moon, lifting their face upwards to allow the acoustics to project their sound. They howl over long distances to defend their territory and communicate during hunting.

January Entertainment

Read:

Black January by Douglas Wynne (2016)

Play:

Last January ~ The Twilight Sad (2014)

January February ~ Barbara Dickson (1980)

Watch:

The January Man (1989)

After a detective is forced to resign due to a scandal, the police reinstate him to help catch a serial killer.

6. PAMPER

Nature dictates January as a time for rest and recuperation, when animals hibernate and seeds focus resources into growing strong roots. We should also take advantage of this respite to pamper body and mind and establish our own roots for a blooming good year ahead!

Think Positive ~ A good place to start is the mind. The brain doesn't care if you are happy as it is wired to protect you, which means it has a natural tendency to give more weight to bad events than good. Training your brain to turn negative thoughts into positive ones is invaluable, as doing so increases the release of feel-good hormones which boosts wellbeing. According to research, regularly practising positive thinking can alter neuron pathways so it eventually becomes second nature!

Learn to be thankful for what you have, no matter how insignificant. Use the phrase 'I get to...' rather than 'I have to...' and try to notice the good things and not dwell on the bad. When you wake, think of three reasons to be grateful and start the day on an optimistic note - I find this really works.

Journal ~ Journals do not follow a chronological order like a diary, they are written in a free form manner which is particularly useful when thoughts race through your mind. Jotting them down and reading them enables you to view any issues from an alternative perspective, which can help you to become more self-aware.

Writing in a journal a few times a week allows you to process and regulate emotions, monitor the progress of objectives and foster a sense of control. Your journal entry can be about whatever springs to mind - observations, dreams, feelings about yourself and others, the past, the future, concerns and challenges. Don't worry about how your writing presents itself as it is for your eyes only - just keep it in a private place.

Listen to Music ~ Music stimulates the brain which can boost mood, mental alertness and memory. Uplifting tunes relieve stress and familiar ones can transport you back to good times in your life. Make the effort to really appreciate your favourites by investing in some noise cancelling headphones. Then get comfy and listen to an album without interruption, from start to finish, and lose yourself in the music.

Rest ~ Begin the weekend the January way with a long leisurely lie in. Waking up and realising that you don't have to jump straight out of your warm bed in the morning is a feeling that's hard to beat. Elevate breakfast in bed with delicious treats and real coffee, then linger in cosy comfort and plan your day ahead.

Breathe ~ Breathing happens automatically but it is useful to understand how changes in breathing pace can impact the body's health. Shallow chest breathing is a typical response to stress which can affect carbon dioxide levels in the body. This may exacerbate anxiety and impact heart rate and blood pressure. A conscious effort to inhale and exhale deep into your belly in a slow controlled manner for a few minutes can trick the brain into a state of calm. This method is highly effective at soothing the body and mind, so practise some simple breathing exercises to stay grounded - one breath at a time!

Walk ~ It is no secret that walking is a great form of exercise. It gets your blood pumping, increases energy levels, burns calories and reduces the risk of conditions, such as high blood pressure. Going for a walk is often synonymous for getting some 'headspace' as studies have shown that the oxygen boost your brain receives helps you to feel calmer and more clear-headed, which is beneficial for mental health. Just remember to go at your own pace.

You may choose some quiet time, or you may prefer company. It is a perfect excuse to connect in a relaxed atmosphere to discuss important issues or chat about nothing in particular. Stop channelling a couch potato and get some colour in your cheeks by wrapping up against the elements and stride out.

Cook ~ Some may argue that cooking for yourself is a chore but I disagree. Taking time to select and prepare nutritious ingredients for a home cooked meal is the ultimate in self-care. Although the focus is on the end result, part of the pleasure is in the process as cooking stimulates your senses which releases endorphins. When your dish is ready to serve, arrange it beautifully on your best plates then raise a glass of something special to celebrate yourself and the delicious dinner you have created - a mini occasion to nourish your body and gladden your soul.

Take a Tech Break ~ Schedule a day without obligations to stay away from all things technological. Put your phone on emergency calls only and place it out of easy reach, then turn off your laptop, TV and radio and live your day. It may feel strange at first but as the hours pass by, your mind will tune into the peace and quiet as you busy yourself with physical activities. Bake, read, clean, walk, craft, eat, snooze - whatever you feel like. After a while the urge to check up on the world will dissipate and you will feel more tranquil and grounded. Remember, the human race survived without technology for a long time - you can cope with one day!

Colour Up ~ When the January blues hit, invest in a colour analysis session to make you look and feel amazing. This technique reveals the colour group that best harmonises with your skin tone to give you a beautiful glow, which is advantageous when choosing clothes or make-up to wear. Try it at home by gathering various coloured garments and place them - one at a time - under your bare face in front of a mirror, in good natural light. If the item draws your eye to itself (instead of your face) and any shadows under your eyes are accentuated, it is not the best colour for you to wear. If the colour brings your gaze to your face, which appears brighter and lifted, then it is one to add to your collection.

Read ~ January is an excellent time to focus on any books you've been meaning to read. Whether it's a story you want to escape into, such as a thriller, or a self-help book to motivate, reading is a great way to relax.

Restock for more cold days ahead by arranging a book swap with friends, browse local charity shops or organise a 'bring one, take one' shelf at work or community centre. Audio books are also excellent to listen to. Close your eyes and lose yourself in another world for a few hours, all while snuggled up safe and sound at home.

Massage ~ Pamper hard working muscles, relieve tension and boost your immune system with a massage. Book yourself into a spa for a treat, coerce your partner into massaging you (and return the favour), or use a portable massage tool and do it yourself! Boost the experience by including aromatherapy oils to ease your mind as well as your body. They are excellent for alleviating symptoms of stress and low mood - always use according to instructions.

Stretch ~ Stress can present as physical pain with tight shoulders, headaches and neck cramps being particularly common, so take time to stretch out any tension in your muscles. This could be a few simple stretches every morning or take it to the next level by doing yoga. Yoga benefits both body and mind as it helps to increase flexibility and strength and relieves anxiety. It is a great way to pamper yourself, can be practised at home or away and offers various levels to keep you challenged and motivated.

Take a Day ~ Imagine waking up knowing you have absolutely nothing to do for a whole day - no chores, no obligations and no work! How would that make you feel and what would you do with the time? Schedule in one day to truly indulge yourself by doing whatever you fancy. Maybe spend it in your comfiest pyjamas, relaxing and pottering at home or head off outdoors for a mini adventure. If you can't manage a whole day then take an afternoon or a 'me'vening to prioritise your pleasure. Enjoy!

JANUARY JOY

Home Spa Day

Spas are great to relieve tension and boost wellbeing but sometimes the travel, communal space and expense can be off putting. A spa in the comfort of your own home can be super tranquil and with a bit of planning, just as luxurious.

Transform your home environment into a spa sanctuary for an indulgent experience. Tidy and warm the bedroom and bathroom and arrange fluffy bath towels, a cosy robe and soft leisure wear for ultimate comfort.

Prepare a refreshing fruit tray and jug of iced water infused with citrus or cucumber slices, to keep you hydrated during your spa time. Set a calming spa vibe with scented candles and soothing music. Select appropriate masks, oils and moisturisers to address any considerations for your skin and hair.

Begin your spa by exfoliating your skin with a dry body brush session - this helps to stimulate collagen production and increase blood flow as well as drain lymph and remove dead skin cells. Use your dry brush in small, firm but gentle motions from your toes to your shoulders, always brushing in the direction of your heart.

Hit the shower and use a gentle exfoliator to get rid of any remaining dead skin cells and use a pumice stone to gently treat rough areas of skin on elbows, knees and feet. Defuzz where you need to and wash your hair using a mild shampoo.

Wrap yourself in your robe and, while you run a warm bath, apply a hair mask to counteract harsh winter effects and leave it feeling silky smooth. Wrap it tightly in a warm towel to keep it in place while the ingredients penetrate. Apply a suitable face mask and allow the warmth of the room to help it seep deep into your pores.

Sink into your bath and soak your cares away. Use bath oils to elevate your experience and let the masks work their magic before rinsing them off. Dry yourself before moisturising from head to toe, then slip into your cosy casuals.

Set to work on a manicure and pedicure and polish your nails in a long-lasting colour to add some January cheer. Finally lay back and enjoy your healthy treats while you spend some time relaxing. Enjoy!

Hug in a Mug – Polish Winter Tea

Making a hot cup of tea can be a reassuring process. Breathing in the soothing aroma and feeling the warmth of the cup in your hands before taking a sip is comforting on a chilly January day.

Polish winters are extremely cold and this winter tea contains vodka, which is perfect for a double hit of heat.

Serves 1. You will need:

1 cup of hot black tea

2 tbsps of raspberry syrup

1 shot of vodka

1 tsp of lemon juice

1 tsp of honey

Method:

Mix the ingredients in a mug and serve while hot. Enjoy!

DID YOU KNOW... that for most of the northern hemisphere, January is the coldest month of the year?

St Hilary's Day on 13th January is traditionally considered the coldest day of the year. St Hilary was raised a pagan but converted to Christianity, eventually becoming Bishop of Poitiers in France, where he died around 367 AD.

The day gained its wintry reputation due to historical records of severe freezing around this date. On 13th January 1205, the Thames River froze over and ale and wine turned to solids, so were sold by weight!

Weather Folklore

Fog in January brings a wet spring.

A favourable January brings us a good year.

If grass grows in January, it will grow badly the whole year.

A summerish January, a winterish spring.

January Entertainment

Read:

January in Atlantis by Alyssa Day (2018)

Play:

January Rain ~ Wynnie Stone (2023)

January White ~ Sleeping at Last (2011)

Watch:

The Two Faces of January (2014)

A scam artist, who works as a tour guide in Greece, is forced to help a couple get away after events take a turn for the worse.

7. DEVELOP

January is regarded by many as a period to get through as quickly as possible, which is a shame as it wastes a whole month of opportunity to stimulate body and mind. Whatever stage of life we are living, we all need something to look forward to so instead of wishing the days away, use this time to develop a new interest and give life a lift.

Practising a hobby or pastime allows you to become absorbed for a while and is a great way to reduce stress, feel motivated and create a sense of achievement.

The experience should be rewarding so choose one which suits your personality and makes you feel good. Find an area you are interested in, maybe something you have always wanted to try - there are plenty of activities for you to consider.

Some involve repetitive movements which can help to soothe you, such as knitting or painting. Others, like cycling, hiking or acting are more energising. Make it as challenging or as chilled as you like.

You may prefer to do a hobby alone, using it as a time to recharge your batteries, or relish getting together with like-minded people to share a passion. A new hobby can bring together those from different cultures, localities and age groups, which offers a chance to make new friends through commonality.

If you want company, join a group or organise one at your local community centre. If you find it tricky to travel to classes, there are plenty of online courses to keep you occupied. Keep hands and minds busy by doing the things you love and time will fly by!

JANUARY JOY

A new and creative activity is great for a sense of emotional balance and wellbeing. There are so many to choose from:

baking ~ collage making ~ hiking ~ gardening ~ cycling ~ photography ~ candle making ~ sewing ~ beach combing ~ embroidery ~ crocheting ~ upcycling ~ foraging ~ reading ~ yoga ~ massage ~ model making ~ pottery ~ flower pressing ~ felting ~ ceramics ~ genealogy ~ soap making ~ calligraphy ~ astrology ~ poetry ~ camping ~ glass fusing ~ kite flying ~ home brewing ~ knitting ~ macramé ~ sculpting ~ bird watching ~ kayaking ~ perfumery ~ acting ~ tapestry ~ wood craft ~ jewellery making ~ drawing ~ painting ~ scrapbooking ~ tie dying ~ fishing ~ creative writing ~ crafting ~ playing an instrument ~ rock balancing ~ chess ~ dancing ~ dominoes ~ surfing ~ backgammon ~ swimming ~ cooking ~ origami ~ geocaching ~ beekeeping ~ aquascaping ~ archery ~ golf ~ decoupage ~ weaving ~ forest bathing ~ soap carving ~ and more!

Hug in a Mug – Chai Latte

Chai latte is a spicy, sweet and creamy hot drink which is one of the oldest tea-based beverages in the world, originating thousands of years ago in India. The spices are infused with the tea and milk which make it fragrant and comforting – delicious on a dreary January morning.

Serves 4. You will need:

2 cinnamon sticks

7 cardamom pods

3 cloves

5 peppercorns

1 star anise

1 inch of ginger, sliced

3 black teabags such as English breakfast tea

500 mls of whole milk or coconut milk

2 tbsps of brown sugar

(cont.)

JANUARY JOY

Method:

Place the cinnamon, cardamom, cloves, peppercorns and star anise in a dry frying pan and heat gently until fragrant.

Transfer to a teapot with the ginger and teabags and add 500 mls of boiled water. Leave for 10 minutes to infuse.

Meanwhile heat the milk. Add the sugar and stir until it has dissolved. When the milk begins to steam, froth it with a whisk or milk frother to create foam.

Strain the tea and pour into 4 mugs. Pour in the milk keeping the froth back, stir, then add the froth to the top. Add a sprinkling of cinnamon if desired.

Enjoy!

DID YOU KNOW... that the birthstone for January is the garnet?

The garnet's name originates from the Latin word 'garanatus' which means 'seedlike' in reference to the similar looking bright red seeds of the pomegranate.

Although the garnet naturally occurs in a range of colours, it is known for its deep red hue. It is an untreated gem made up of many minerals and symbolises constancy, truth and faith.

The garnet is incredibly durable with beads found as far back as 3000 B.C. According to history, Plato had his portrait engraved on one and the Anglo Saxons had many items of jewellery set with garnets. The gemstone was popular in Europe in the 18th and 19th century due to its rarity, colour and lustre.

The garnet is surrounded by folklore and was considered a protective talisman, worn for strength, endurance and attractiveness.

January Entertainment

Read:

The January Queen by Joyce Stranger (1979)

Play:

January ~ Elton John (1997)

The Month of January ~ June Tabor (1983)

Watch:

June in January (2014)

A newly engaged bride has her dreams threatened by her future mother-in-law as her June wedding date is changed to January.

8. EXPLORE

Freezing weather conditions and seasonal coughs and sneezes may make staying in seem very appealing but getting out of the house, even for a short time, can make the day feel much more productive. Prevent January 'sofa slump' by going outside to explore!

The restorative power of travel is well known. A pleasant trip away can help lower stress and boost creativity, health and happiness. Just the anticipation of a new adventure can be beneficial as it releases feel good hormones which stimulate and invigorate. The weather may be dreary but begin to plan a trip away and notice how much better you feel.

If a holiday is not an option, then a few days away is the next best thing. Keep your eyes open for any travel deals happening after the festive season. Consider a cultural city break, a spa weekend or a little time relaxing at a remote woodland cabin. If on a budget, a house swap with trusted friends who live in a different area to you is highly recommended!

Experience a little winter magic by travelling out of the city and suburbs. The UK has breathtaking landscapes which support all sorts of unique wildlife. Cornwall offers miles and miles of dramatic coastlines and the historic New Forest is a great place for spotting ponies and deer. Step back in time by visiting charming York which is close to the Yorkshire Dales and Moors - perfect for exhilarating hikes.

The Cotswolds provide pretty as a picture cottages and meandering lanes and the Lake District is a sight to behold with its lakes, fells and snow-capped peaks. Norfolk offers plenty of opportunity for bird watching on tranquil flat lands and salt marshes. Head to the Scottish Highlands for lochs and magnificent mountains and maybe an eagle or two, or spend a couple of days enjoying the vast beachscapes and wild woodlands of Wales.

If you need to stay close to home then plan some exciting days out. Wrap up against the elements, gather a hot picnic (soup and a pasty is always a winner) and immerse yourself in your local environment. Watch your breath evaporate in the cold air as you spot birds, deer, wildfowl, hares, otters and squirrels in their natural surroundings. Check out the National Trust to see what is on your doorstep.

If hiking through the countryside isn't your thing, then why not explore your local town or city and check out delicious fooderies on route. Visit historical monuments - including the pubs. They are a valued part of the British landscape and provide the perfect excuse to recuperate with a cheeky drink and some hearty fayre before heading home.

Take a look at theatres, concerts and shows happening near you, including matinee performances if you don't want to be out late. Dress up and make it an occasion. A laugh is good for the soul so seek out a stand-up comedy event or be brave and try entertaining the crowd yourself on an 'open mic' evening.

If you want to challenge your brain and get the adrenalin pumping then book an escape room experience. Grab a team and have fun testing your problem-solving skills while unravelling riddles and deciphering codes against the clock, before celebrating or commiserating afterwards.

Hug in a Mug – Hot Toddy

The hot toddy has evolved over time into a delicious drink remedy which will warm you from top to toe. For a non-alcoholic version, swap the whisky for black tea.

Serves 2. You will need:

50 mls of whisky

3 tsps of honey

2 cinnamon sticks and 2 cloves

Juice of ½ a lemon and two wedges of lemon

Method:

Add the honey to the whisky in a small bowl and whisk. Divide between two mugs, add a cinnamon stick to each then top up with boiling water.

Share the lemon juice between the mugs then press a clove into each lemon wedge and pop into the mugs. Enjoy!

DID YOU KNOW... that January has two birth flowers - the carnation and the snowdrop?

Carnation (Dianthus caryophyllus)

Carnations are native to the Mediterranean and have been cultivated for over two thousand years. The ancient Greeks and Romans used them at festivals and ceremonies for floral decorations.

The name carnation stems from the Latin word carnis, meaning flesh, referring to their original pink shade, or from corona which means crown - due to Greek coronations. The word dianthus translates from Greek as divine flower.

Their pretty ruffled petals emit a sweet fragrance which bloom in the late spring and early summer.

Carnations signify love and affection yet the colour 'code' for carnations should be noted when sending them to others! Light red conveys admiration, dark red imparts deep love, white expresses pure love and pink reveals admiration or affection. Purple communicates capriciousness, yellow states disappointment and striped indicates rejection!

Snowdrop (Galanthus nivalis)

This delicate bell-shaped white flower blooms from bulbs in late winter and early spring, even in the snow. They are native to Europe and Western Asia.

The name Galanthus nivalis, which means 'milk flower of the snow' is derived from the Greek words gala (milk) and anthos (flower). The species name 'nivalis' translates as 'of the snow'.

Its medicinal properties were applied to relieve fever and pain. Some species contain galantamine which has been used to treat cognitive disorders.

Snowdrops symbolise hope, resilience and renewal. In Victorian times they represented purity and were also used to ward off evil spirits and bring good luck.

January Entertainment

Read:

January 3rd ½ by Debora S. Davis (2002)

Play:

January ~ Loving (2020)

January Rain ~ Hunters and Collectors (1986)

Watch:

The Night of January 16th (1941)

Everyone suspects a rich man has been murdered by his secretary, yet despite mounting evidence against her, she maintains her innocence.

9. CONNECT

Although January is a great time to focus on self-care, it is also valuable to stay in touch with others. Contact is a basic human need but at this time of year, when the rain falls and socialising takes a back seat, our world may become a little smaller. Make the effort to connect with others for some fun and affection.

Get Together!

Maintaining positive relationships helps to satisfy the soul. You are affected by who you spend your time with so prioritise connecting with those who have your best interests at heart and reap the benefits of each other's support.

If you live far apart, take turns to travel for catch ups by the fire, or plan a day out somewhere stimulating, such as an art gallery or nature trail walk.

Remember to cherish those you spend your 'every-days' with. Family may be familiar like part of the furniture but instead of taking them for granted, make time to delight in each other's company. Movie nights snuggled up on the sofa, delicious meals prepared together and long winter walks arm in arm, are all memories made.

Food, Glorious Food ~ Food not only sustains, it draws people together. It's good to chat over coffee and cake, or spend an afternoon cooking a tasty dish with others. Teaching a young one to bake biscuits or organising a 'Come Dine With Me' experience with like-minded companions can be fun. If you are on your own, join a cooking group and make some new foodie friends.

Experience the taste of far-away cultures without leaving your home by preparing a foreign feast for your family to enjoy. If you love all things Spanish, begin your evening with a jug of sangria or a bottle of rioja with tasty tomato bread.

Follow with a traditional main course and dessert, such as paella and Leche Frita. Make some Spanish table decorations, play Spanish tunes and follow up with a Spanish film.

There are so many themes to choose from - try Spicy Thai, Fabulous French, Hot Mexican, Super Scandi or Awesome Aussie!

Game On ~ Regular playtime supports good mental health as it releases endorphins, improves cognitive skills, counteracts stress and contributes to social wellbeing and healthier relationships. Channel your inner child by getting together to play childhood favourites, such as Operation, Scrabble, Connect 4 or Risk. Unleash your competitive side and organise a charades tournament or retro computer game session of Pac-Man, Street Fighter or Donkey Kong. If it is tricky to physically get together, arrange a virtual games night online.

Party Up ~ Hosting a party in January can really brighten the month and it doesn't have to be expensive. A clothes swap event can be rewarding at this time of year. Search through your wardrobe for pieces you no longer love and get satisfaction seeing them find a new home - while you acquire some lovely new items for yourself. See the **Celebrate** section for plenty of excuses to have a good time!

Love ~ January is an ideal month to reconnect with your partner, so schedule in some special time for just the two of you. Try something simple, such as a wine and cheese carpet picnic in front of the fire with candles and relaxing music, or treat yourselves to a meal out together, somewhere special. Chat about where you want this year to take you - both individually and as a couple - and plan some exciting new adventures. Anticipation of good times ahead can really help to strengthen your bond and reawaken your appreciation for each other.

Make New Friends!

Sometimes circumstances, such as moving house to a new area or being naturally shy, may mean connecting with others can be challenging. Taking positive action to deal with these issues is important as long-term loneliness has been found to negatively affect health. The saying 'There are no strangers; only friends we haven't met yet' shows every first meeting has potential. Be brave and use January to dip your toe into a new social pool.

Never Compare ~ When we compare our lives to others (particularly through social media) it can be easy to fall into the trap of feeling inadequate. This is a slippery slope and should be avoided. Remember that other people's lives are seldom as they seem, so wasting hours of time evaluating your life against picture-perfect posts is not helpful - don't do it!

Let Go ~ If friendships are not being nurtured or you regularly feel dissatisfied after spending time in their company, it is ok to let them go - with love. Maybe they have changed, maybe you have changed, but if you feel they don't make any effort to listen to you or are only there for the good times, bid a fond farewell and use your energy to develop a friendship circle of more genuine connections.

Appreciate You ~ You are your own best friend. Spending time alone doesn't mean you have to feel lonely. Explore ways to boost self-esteem by pampering yourself or learning something new. If you do feel isolated then consider welcoming a pet into your life. It is amazing how another living being in the home can influence mood in such a positive way.

Get Out There ~ Friends are made early in life through shared experiences but as time goes on, making new companions can become a lower priority. All friendships begin with an element of chance, so think about what you would like from a new connection and the best place to meet them. Find a positive environment where you can meet people with common interests and see how you respond to each other. Make sure that you appear friendly and approachable, be receptive to small talk and if it doesn't go the way you hoped, accept it and move on. It's not just about luck, it is also about perseverance and building confidence in yourself.

Consider Acquaintances ~ Some believe forming genuine friendships become more difficult with age, but it is also worth remembering that many are in a similar position. There are many acquaintances which have the potential to blossom into friendship if you take that extra step! Suggest a coffee or beer with someone you'd like to get to know better - perhaps a work colleague, a fellow dog walker or a friendly neighbour.

Community Spirit ~ Make the most of your locality by connecting with others. Check out classes at your leisure centre or try joining a local interest group - maybe art, hiking or drama. A book club is good to get to know people as it encourages discussion of various points of view, or just become a regular at your local coffee shop and get your face known.

Volunteer ~ Expand your world by helping others. Not only does it enable you to put your own troubles into perspective, it also provides purpose, creates opportunities to meet generous minded people and boosts self-esteem. Offer your time at a local fundraising charity, homeless shelter, food bank or hospital and make a difference.

Friends Online ~ If you feel hesitant about physically meeting new people, try the virtual approach. Talking to others through social app groups and online forums means you can dip in and out of conversations as you please without any pressure of long-term commitment. Providing it is done safely, it provides an opportunity to chat to like-minded people of different ages and backgrounds from all over the world, which may lead to meaningful friendships over time.

More Than Friendship!

Date ~ If you want to meet someone special, January is a good time to take the first step. Local dating groups may be a good option or consider online dating websites which have plenty of members and cater to all personality types. Many offer the chance to chat virtually before meeting face to face. Remember to stay safe and have fun!

Safe Online Dating

Choose a reputable dating platform by checking out dating site reviews online.

If you feel uncomfortable during an interaction, be aware and explore it. Do not excuse unacceptable behaviour.

NEVER share your passwords or financial information. If they ask, report them and move on.

Before meeting face to face, vet the person with a video call to make sure they are who they say they are.

Always arrange meetings in a busy public place and ensure you have suitable transport to get home.

Tell your friends, family or a trusted neighbour where you are going and who you are meeting.

Maintain a safe boundary while you get to know them better. Do not follow each other on social media or share personal information, phone numbers, home addresses or intimate photos.

Hug in a Mug - Mulled Wine

Infuse your home throughout January with the wonderful spicy aroma of mulled wine. Add the preferred wine of your choice so it is exactly to your liking.

Serves 6. You will need:

Peel from an unwaxed lemon and 2 unwaxed oranges

75g of caster sugar

3 cloves, 1 star anise and 1 cinnamon stick

A pinch of ground nutmeg and ground ginger

1 bottle of fruity red wine

Method:

Thinly slice the oranges, add to a saucepan with the wine, spices and lemon peel then heat and stir gently. Add the sugar, bring to the boil then reduce the heat and simmer for five minutes. Strain into mugs and serve with a cooked orange slice. Enjoy!

JANUARY JOY

DID YOU KNOW... that the zodiac signs which occur in January are Capricorn and Aquarius?

Capricorn reigns from December 22nd to January 19th and Aquarius - January 20th to February 18$^{th.}$

The zodiac personalities are complete opposites with Capricorn tending to be stubborn and steadfast, like the goat that represents the sign. Aquarians are generally more relaxed, possessing a 'go with the flow' attitude, symbolic of the water carrier.

Famous January birthdays include Elvis Presley, Dolly Parton, Gary Barlow, The Princess of Wales, Alicia Keys and Nic Cage. Research suggests that there is a connection between babies born in January and the likelihood of becoming a professional athlete or CEO.

In numerology, those born in January are ruled by the number 1, tend to be independent and analytical, and have potential to become high achievers.

January Entertainment

Read:

January Fifteenth by Rachel Swirsky (2022)

Play:

January Thaw ~ Chip Harding (2022)

January ~ Millie Turner (2019)

Watch:

January (2021)

In the midst of nowhere, five men are stuck in a snow storm and the wolves are hungry!

10. CELEBRATE

Celebrating is not just about creating opportunities for fun and entertainment - it is also good for our physical and mental wellbeing. What a great excuse to celebrate!

The act of celebrating can be beneficial for physical health as it facilitates excitement and activity which can release feel-good hormones and get the blood pumping.

Mental health can also benefit as when we celebrate, we are reinforcing something which is meaningful to us, which activates the brain's reward system - boosting self-esteem and motivation. It leaves us in a buoyant state of mind resulting from a sense of accomplishment and satisfaction.

In addition, having a good time with others helps to strengthen emotional bonds, enhances social skills, creates memories and generates a positive vibe. It demonstrates to those who we choose to gather with, that they are valued, which nurtures a sense of belonging.

While making the most of this period to rest and recuperate, we should also take a little time to enjoy ourselves. Embrace January and all of its quirks by celebrating International Days from around the world. There are so many to choose from - select a few that appeal to you and your loved ones and have fun! Here are my personal favourites which bring me January Joy!

Swiss Cheese Day ~ January 2nd

Swiss Cheese Day is held to celebrate the delicious cheese which originated hundreds of years ago when the people of Switzerland began making their own cheese around the 14th century. Over time it adapted to become more popular and is now famous across the globe and loved by people everywhere. It even has its own festival!

The distinctive look of Swiss cheese is due to carbon dioxide producing bubbles in the cheese which forms holes. It is one of the healthiest cheeses to eat with relatively low levels of fat, lactose and sodium and is full of calcium, vitamin B12, protein and zinc. It has a mild sweet and nutty flavour and tastes great in sandwiches, salads, soups and chicken dishes. Popular varieties include Emmental, Gruyere and Appenzeller.

Celebrate the day by inviting your nearest and dearest to share a Swiss cheese fondue.

Swiss Cheese Fondue

Serves 4-6

For the fondue dip you will need:

200g of Gruyere, grated

100g of Gouda, grated

100g of Emmental, grated

2 tbsps of cornstarch

200 mls of dry white wine

1 clove of garlic minced (optional)

1 tbsp of freshly squeezed lemon juice

1 tbsp of brandy

1 tsp of Dijon mustard

A pinch of ground nutmeg

(cont.)

For the fondue dippers you will need:

Crusty bread, cut into bite size chunks

Steamed new potatoes

Lightly steamed broccoli heads and asparagus spears

Cornichons

Cooked sausage, cut into bite sized chunks

Cherry tomatoes

Method:

Place the grated cheeses with the cornstarch into a bowl and combine well. Using a large saucepan, add the wine, garlic and lemon juice and bring to a simmer.

Add the cheeses to the saucepan little by little, stirring well. When the mixture is smooth add the brandy, mustard and nutmeg and stir well.

Arrange the fondue dippers onto a platter, pour the dip into a fondue pot over a flame and serve immediately with fondue forks and napkins. Enjoy!

Festival of Sleep Day ~ January 3rd

If you enjoy your zzz's, you will love Festival of Sleep Day! Its creator remains a mystery but the anticipation of slipping under cosy covers before drifting into the land of nod is relished by many at this time of year - to help recover from New Year festivities.

Lack of sleep can be detrimental to health. Tiredness can impair cognitive processes such as concentration which may cause accidents, and long-term sleep deprivation can lead to heart and blood pressure problems. Yet, in our modern world where technology offers artificial light and online entertainment at any hour, sleep deficiency is common.

Celebrate this day by acknowledging the benefits of a good night's sleep and take some time to improve your sleeping environment. Ensure your bedroom is sleep suitable - that it allows you to wind down without distraction and is an appropriate temperature. Treat yourself to new pyjamas and bedding, consider a contemporary mattress and resolve to reduce unnecessary late nights.

Sweet dreams!

JANUARY JOY

International Choreographers Day ~ January 9th

Dance has evolved over thousands of years, fostered by an innate desire to move to the rhythm. The word choreographer comes from Greek which literally translates to 'dance writing'.

From Hollywood spectaculars to Bollywood extravaganzas - it is the skills of numerous choreographers that helped create them. So, whether you prefer the fancy footwork routines of live musical theatre or get a thrill from cutting-edge music video moves, put on your dancing shoes and show appreciation for all those who have helped the world to be entertained by dance.

Celebrate the day by learning about famous choreographers, such as Bob Fosse who was a pioneer for jazz dance, George Balanchine who co-founded the New York city ballet, Agnes de Mille who helped transform 1940s and 1950s American musical theatre and Gene Kelly who strove to make dance accessible to the general public.

Get active and copy some great dance moves. It could be the infamous New Year's Eve dance routine from *Friends* (1999, S6 E10), John Travolta's 'Far from Over' in *Staying Alive* (1983) or Jennifer Beal's 'What a Feeling' from *Flashdance* (1983).

When you need a rest from high kicks and pirouettes, treat yourself by booking tickets to a musical or settle down to watch some great film choreography. Try *Singin' in the Rain* (1952) with Gene Kelly and Debbie Reynolds, *West Side Story* (1961) with Natalie Wood and Richard Beymer, *La La Land* (2016) with Ryan Gosling and Emma Stone, *Dirty Dancing* (1987) with Patrick Swayze and Jennifer Grey or *The Red Shoes* (1948) with Moira Shearer - they are all fantastic.

International Thank You Day ~ January 11th

Saying thank you is a common daily occurrence for most people. International Thank You Day provides an ideal opportunity to show your appreciation to those who have had a positive impact on your life. It could be a colleague who is supportive at work, a friend who helped you at a difficult time or a neighbour who looks out for you. It is a day that stimulates joy and is also a reminder to be kind to others.

There are various ways to express your thanks. Send a handmade thank you card with a personal message written inside or create a heartfelt video - imagine their surprise when they receive it! Plan a delicious thank you meal by cooking their favourite dish or treat them to coffee and cake somewhere special.

If you have many people to thank, throw a surprise party for them all. Guarantee great vibes with thank you cupcakes, fun games, a playlist of their favourite songs and a bottle or two of fizz.

Use the day to pay the thanks forward by helping out those in need in your community - raise charity funds for veterans or volunteer at your local hospital.

Make Your Dream Come True Day ~ January 13th

Do you dream of owning a house by the sea, travelling the world or running your own business? Instead of letting it fade away, use this day to take the first step towards turning your dream into reality. With some careful planning, plenty of persistence and a little courage, who knows what you may achieve!

It doesn't matter how big your dream is, the key is to split it into manageable chunks in order to get closer to reaching your goal. Share this day with a friend to motivate and support each other's aspirations - sometimes two heads are better than one.

Maybe you have always dreamed of living in another country for a year to absorb the culture and learn the language. Calculate the cost, work out a long-term budget then approach your manager to discuss the possibility of taking a sabbatical in the future, or consider the steps to gaining short term employment over there.

Motivate yourself by reading some of the numerous self-help books available, which focus on how to make dreams come true. Take time to watch a film that will inspire you to follow your dreams. Try *The Shawshank Redemption* (1994), *High Noon* (1952), *Cool Runnings* (1993), *The Pursuit of Happyness* (2006), *Field of Dreams* (1989), *Jerry Maguire* (1996) and *Soul Surfer* (2011).

International Kite Day ~ January 14th

Let's go fly a kite - that is what this day is all about! Weather permitting, choose a colourful kite then get outside and breathe in the fresh air while you watch it flutter, dip and dive in the sky.

It is thought that the kite originated in China more than two thousand years ago with the legend of a farmer who struggled to keep his hat on in the wind. To stop it blowing away he attached it to a string and when it blew off his head again, it became the first 'kite'.

International Kite Day originated in India - the country has paintings that show kites from around five hundred years ago. The Gujarat state hosts the kite festival which is celebrated on the day that their winter ends and summer begins. The kites represent spirits of the gods awakening from their deep sleep of winter and are made months in advance as the festival is very popular, with millions visiting from around the world.

Celebrate the day by taking your kite out and enjoy the challenge of keeping it high in the sky! Go one step further and create your own - it could be a traditional diamond kite, a box kite or stunt kite. Decorate it to your liking, send it soaring and enjoy feeling like a kid again!

International Hot and Spicy Food Day ~ January 16th

Do you like it hot - your food I mean? If you do, then International Hot and Spicy Food Day is the ideal time to feed your passion with a culinary spice explosion. Celebrations generally involve chilli eating challenges and spicy cook offs, with the Scoville heat scale playing a large part.

Use this day to appreciate how spices used for thousands of years, such as chilli, cumin, turmeric and paprika, have added flavour to our diet and provided health benefits, due to their powerful anti-inflammatory, antioxidant and antimicrobial properties.

If you prefer tongue tingles to watering eyes, take control of the heat by cooking up a spicy themed night for loved ones to suit various tastes. Prepare Indian, Creole, Chinese or Thai recipes and let the spicy aromas infuse your kitchen, just be sure to have some natural yoghurt or cold milk to cool the palate if needed.

Brew Monday ~ 3rd Monday in January

Brew Monday is a practical approach to making a positive difference for those who struggle with the winter blues. It was created in response to 'Blue Monday' which surfaced in 2005 as a result of a travel company publicity campaign. The marketing gimmick was based on a psychological 'formula' which used various factors, such as weather, resolution success, time since Christmas day and financial debt, to come to a theoretical conclusion that this day was the most depressing of the year.

The good news is that Blue Monday is now the date when the initiative Brew Monday focuses on those who struggle with their mental health at this time of year. It is a day to check in and provide care for those who may need it, as well as recognising any symptoms yourself and understanding the importance of talking about them with your healthcare provider.

Transform Blue Monday to Brew Monday by hosting a community event. Provide tea, coffee, cake and conversation and raise awareness and funds for charities which focus on mental wellbeing.

Let's all raise our teacups to that!

Good Memory Day ~ January 19th

At the end of the day, memories are all that we really have and we owe it to ourselves to make plenty of good ones. Happy experiences should be cherished as their recall has the power to give us a mental boost. Celebrate this day by putting aside any worries about the future and focus on reminiscing about joyous occasions from your past instead!

It could be anything from winning a competition, meeting your true love, the day your baby was born, fun times with friends, a wonderful holiday, buying your first car or a party you had as a child. Take time to really think about it in detail and relive all the positive emotions that went with it.

Go a step further on your walk down memory lane and make a scrap book full of items of nostalgia which you may have kept, e.g. concert tickets, photos and postcards. Write a description next to them of what was happening and how it made you feel.

Another aspect of Good Memory Day is realising that training your memory is important as you get older - as the saying goes 'use it or lose it'. Incorporate memory exercises into your daily routine by learning a foreign language or musical instrument. Take time to memorise phone numbers and use a memory test app.

Penguin Awareness Day ~ January 20th

Penguins are fascinating creatures and are worth celebrating. They have been around for over sixty-five million years and are a stoic breed of eighteen different species. Unfortunately, their number is dwindling at an alarming rate and scientists worldwide are striving to highlight the predicament of the penguins and promote their conservation. Use this day to learn all about them and their environment.

Visit a penguin sanctuary and take the opportunity to get up close. Watch a documentary about them and research where you can help their cause. The Global Penguin Society is the first international organisation committed solely to penguin conservation.

Discover their efforts to reduce encroachment of their feeding grounds and control depletion of fishing stock. You can even help by adopting a penguin!

All penguins live in the southern hemisphere.

Their feathers and body fat enable them to endure the harshest climates.

Unlike other birds, penguins have solid bones to help them dive fast through water.

Penguins make paths through ice to collect food more easily but can be picky with their food, eating mainly krill and fish to stay healthy.

A group of penguins in water is called a raft.

A group of penguins on land is called a waddle.

They can walk for up to 100km to reach their destination.

International Sweatpants Day ~ January 21st

We all love to slip into something more comfortable to relax but International Sweatpants Day gives us the excuse to do it all day long!

Initially named 'jogging bottoms', sweatpants were invented in the 1920s by founder of Le Coq Sportif - Émile Camuset - for athletes to keep muscles warm between competitions.

They became popular by the late 1970s and were upgraded in the mid-2000s when incorporated into high end fashion lines, with iconic logos and designs. By 2010, the development of the athleisure trend led to a huge increase in their popularity and sweatpants are now available in many materials and styles.

Apparently, the idea to celebrate sweatpants began in the early 2000s by a group of students. Honour the day by wearing your favourites to lounge around in, treat yourself to a new pair and donate your old ones or upgrade a current pair with beads, paint and patches.

Have a party in your sweatpants by inviting friends around for a competition of the funniest, cutest or most 'tragic' pair. Serve French drinks and snacks in honour of Camuset and his brilliant invention.

Finally, watch a movie featuring sweatpants while relaxing in your comfiest pair - perhaps *Rocky 2* (1979) with Sylvester Stallone.

International Sticky Toffee Pudding Day ~ January 23rd

This is a perfect day to treat your tastebuds by indulging in a slice of sticky toffee pudding!

The traditional British pudding has a unique flavour which is the result of the moist sponge cake containing dates, and the toffee sauce including black treacle. The story of its exact origin is unclear although it traces back to the early 1900s. One version claims a chef forgot to include sugar when baking a sponge cake, so he improvised by using dates and syrup to add sweetness.

However it came to be, this delicious and gooey pudding we know and love has been a firm favourite with the British for many years. By the 1990s, the dessert gained recognition internationally with renowned restaurants adding it to their menu. A decade later it became available on supermarket shelves for the general public to purchase and enjoy at home.

Celebrate this day by getting together with loved ones to bake a sticky toffee pudding from scratch - it is delicious served with cream, ice cream or custard. Experiment with different recipe variations or concoct your own and vote for the tastiest. Instead of dates you could try nuts, instead of toffee sauce use crème anglaise.

If you don't fancy baking, buy one to share with a friend - you'll be glad you did and so will they!

Global Belly Laugh Day ~ January 24th

Gelotology (from the Greek 'gelos' for laughter) is the study of laughter and its psychological and physiological effects on the body.

Laughter is said to be the best medicine. It encourages a lighter perspective, distracts us from everyday issues and makes us feel great. Research has shown the link between laughing and the relief of tension in the body, better memory and sleep quality. It can also stimulate a healthier immune system and is associated with increased life satisfaction.

Laughter is an important part of human communication as it helps us to bond with others and has been used in several types of treatment, including Humour Therapy, Laughter Yoga and Laughter Meditation.

Use this day to harness the power of a deep belly laugh. Try to remember something that had you in stitches, meet up with a friend who is a hoot, watch your favourite comedy programme, get tickled, swap jokes with family, find something hilarious online or watch a live comedy performance.

Find your funny - it will keep you upbeat for the rest of the day and your mind and body will love you for it!

Burns Night ~ January 25th

Burns Night is a well-known celebration which is held each year on the 25th January in recognition of Scotland's beloved poet, Robert Burns. Born in January 1759, Burns penned hundreds of poems which captured the life and spirit of everyday Scottish people, until his death in 1796. However, his poem 'Auld Lang Syne', which is typically sung at midnight on New Year's Eve, is arguably the most famous.

Formal celebrations are held all over the country with a Burns supper, whisky tasting, poetry reading, Scottish music played on bagpipes, fiddles, harp and guitars and a traditional Scottish dance known as a ceilidh (pronounced 'kay-lee').

Celebrations are not complete until the gathered raise their glasses to the haggis and pay tribute to the great Scot with a toast - *Slàinte Mhath!* (pronounced 'slan-cha va!'). It is also common to read the 17th century Scottish prayer '*Selkirk Grace*' before the haggis is 'piped in'. It gives thanks for the meal and was attributed to Burns after he recited it at a dinner party, although he did not write it;

Some hae meat and canna eat,

And some wad eat that want it;

But we hae meat, and we can eat,

Sae let the Lord be thankit.

Celebrate Burns Night at home by draping your dinner table with tartan, cook up a feast of haggis, neeps and tatties (turnips and potatoes) and cranachan - a delicious Scottish dessert. Then sample a tot or two of whisky before playing Scottish music and trying your footwork at *'The Gay Gordons'* - usually the first dance at a ceilidh.

Australia Day ~ January 26th

Australia Day is a great excuse to celebrate everything which is Aussie. Australia is a country and continent filled with both beauty and danger. It has amazing beaches and merciless deserts, cute koalas and deadly spiders and laid-back citizens with a fierce pride.

The Australians celebrate their day with festivals, fireworks, barbeques and open-air events but you don't need to live there to be part of it. Learn about its history and how it has progressed to be one of the world's wealthiest countries.

Celebrate the day by speaking a little Aussie; G'day (hello), hooroo (goodbye), bonzer (excellent), ripper (cool), stoked (happy or excited) and fair dinkum (genuine).

Cook Australian cuisine, a delicious fusion of European and Asian influences with indigenous bush foods and seafood from the oceans that surround it. It also has a thriving wine industry so treat yourself to a bottle of its finest!

Finally, settle down with a few famous Australians! Watch films featuring Heath Ledger, Hugh Jackman, Chris and Liam Hemsworth, Toni Collette and Cate Blanchett. Listen to Australian singers and bands, including AC/DC, Crowded House, Midnight Oil, Tame Impala, Men at Work, Nick Cave, Empire of the Sun, INXS and Kylie Minogue.

Inspire Your Heart with Art Day ~ January 31st

Art is crucial for the expression of the human spirit and this is the day to celebrate it. From cave paintings to digital art and everything in between, our desire to create and stimulate has been revealed throughout the ages.

Lack of art has been shown to negatively impact the mental and emotional health of adults and children alike, so be sure to embrace your own artistic vibe with something that inspires your heart.

Explore the creations of others by taking time to browse an art gallery, watch an independent film, go to the theatre to see a thought-provoking play or admire new collections at a fashion show.

Creating art enables you to convey your emotions and boost self-esteem through a sense of accomplishment. Design a piece of artwork which expresses your personality and imagination with a medium that suits you, e.g. clay, paint, fabric, dance, mime, music or pen.

DAILY MOOD BOOSTS

Most of us experience the odd day when the world seems a little less friendly, or negative emotions take centre stage.

The good news is we can do something about it!

When you are feeling down, agitated or bored, set aside a little time to alter your current mindset.

The following mood boosts always lift my spirits and I hope they do the same for you.

Take one each January day!

MOOD BOOST 1

Watch a winter movie!

On a dreary day, when the rain hammers against the window, we could do a lot worse than hunker down under a warm blanket with a bowl of freshly made popcorn, and become totally absorbed in a movie!

Embrace January by choosing from the following freezing films:

Everest (2015)

Groundhog Day (1993)

Frozen (2013)

The Revenant (2015)

The Thing (1982)

Snow Dogs (2002)

The Day After Tomorrow (2004)

The Mountain Between Us (2017)

By the end of it, you'll appreciate how lucky you are to have a warm and cosy home. If you don't have time for a film, watch an episode of a binge worthy series but be warned as they are addictive!

Here are my favourite snowy options:

Fortitude, Fargo, Vikings, Spinning Out, Snowpiercer and *Alone*.

MOOD BOOST 2
Think happy!

By January many of us feel like the winter will never end. Fortunately, the subconscious mind doesn't realise the difference between dreams and reality. When we shut our eyes and imagine something lovely, such as walking along a sunny beach with the sea lapping at our toes, our brain releases serotonin which gives the body a boost.

Support a capacity for happiness by letting in those joyful thoughts. Bask in fond memories of fun times with friends, intimate moments with your loved ones, belly laughs with your bestie, amazing places you have visited or moments of success - anything that elevates your mood.

Take it a step further by writing a list of things that bring you pleasure and aim to do a few every week. My January joy comes from taking time to… paint a picture, watch a band, bake bread, hike somewhere new, drink cocktails with friends, call a loved one, relax in a bubble bath, have breakfast in bed, go out for dinner, watch a movie, visit an animal sanctuary, walk on the beach, order pizza, have a massage, listen to great music, read a good book, eat chocolate ice cream, chill with my dog, play cards and help someone in need!

MOOD BOOST 3
Light a candle!

Candlelight is beneficial for wellbeing as it emits a low light which supports relaxation. A candle flame enables us to move from a 'reactive beta' to a 'relaxed alpha' brainwave state which helps us to feel soothed.

The gentle glow from a candle flame provides a comforting, meditative and peaceful environment which can help to lower stress levels, reduce irritation, boost immunity and improve sleep quality.

Large or small, scented or unscented, coloured or natural - choose a candle to suit your mood and enjoy its effect. I find lighting one with breakfast and dinner in January creates a cosy and harmonious vibe.

Always ensure you burn it within sight and extinguish the flame safely.

MOOD BOOST 4
Alter the aroma!

Our sense of smell has the ability to strongly impact the activity of the brain as it directly influences areas that process emotion. We all know how an aroma can transport us back to the time it was first experienced - my perfume still has the power to take me back to my teenage years!

Fragrances have the ability to alter mood by triggering feel-good hormones, as well as making the home smell fabulous. For an instant lift, use an essential oil diffuser spray and take time to enjoy the effects.

Here are some of my favourites:

Lavender helps to control stress and improve sleep.
Jasmine soothes anxiety and boosts optimism.
Neroli reduces stress levels.
Rose contains anti-anxiety agents.
Lemon calms and clarifies and supports immunity.
Rosemary has stimulating properties and improves memory.
Peppermint is invigorating and provides clarity.

Always use according to instructions.

MOOD BOOST 5
Do a good deed!

Performing random acts of kindness not only helps others, it can also benefit the person doing it. Helping someone down on their luck provides a welcome distraction from our own problems and can produce a 'helpers high' - creating a positive effect on wellbeing.

Research has shown that the more we are kind to others, the more it can become second nature which can significantly boost self-esteem.

Raising good deed awareness in the community is valuable in many ways. It demonstrates that there are decent people out there, helping those in need for nothing in return, which can inspire others to join in and spread even more positivity and kindness.

There are many ways to accomplish acts of kindness. Doing something as simple as opening the door for a stranger, paying a compliment or helping a person cross the road is significant and can make their day. If you want to do more, volunteering to work for a local charity can be extremely worthwhile.

Do a good deed and everyone wins!

MOOD BOOST 6
Do a jigsaw puzzle!

On a dreary January day, it is lovely to get cosy and spend time doing a jigsaw puzzle, but did you know that it is also good for our health?

Becoming absorbed in a jigsaw puzzle keeps us focused on the present which helps to ease stress and reduce blood pressure. Fitting the pieces together allows the hormone dopamine to be released - which induces a sense of satisfaction. It also improves fine motor skills, problem-solving ability, short term memory, brain agility and reduces screen time.

Jigsaw puzzles are good to do alone or with others as they are an easy way to spend time together, which can encourage bonding. There are many types to choose from as they come in plenty of different shapes and sizes with various difficulty levels. Popular ones include picturesque landscapes and seascapes, famous paintings, cute animals, world maps, repetitive patterns (really tricky) and 3D form.

Set up a dedicated jigsaw puzzle space at home to tempt those passing by to give it a try. It's always a nice surprise to find a few more pieces have been completed. For young children, set up an age-appropriate jigsaw next to the adult puzzle to make them feel part of the team.

MOOD BOOST 7

Make a happiness jar!

Good and bad things happen every day but the brain tends to focus on the negative - not 'how nice my friend paid me a compliment', more 'why did my colleague roll their eyes at me?'.

A happiness jar is an exercise which helps to rewire the brain to acknowledge the everyday wins. It encourages appreciation of good moments and can enhance our sense of gratitude and perspective.

Write down something which brought you happiness on a small piece of paper, fold it up and place it in a jar for safe keeping - bright coloured post it notes are ideal. It could be a neighbour paying you a compliment, a smile from a stranger, passing an exam, reaching the summit on a mountain hike, your boss appreciating the work you do, flowers from a friend or a loved one cooking a delicious meal for you.

As time goes by and your notes build up, read them and remember the many moments of joy you experienced but have probably forgotten. If you are always on the go, make a virtual happiness jar on your phone.

Dip into your happiness jar any time you need some positivity in your life, or save it for a special occasion. Refresh it every year or keep it going until it becomes a huge happiness jar!

MOOD BOOST 8
Write a letter!

In these days of digital, writing a traditional letter using pen and paper is considered old fashioned. However, it is the sentiment that counts - it is a heartfelt way to show a friend that we appreciate them.

The gesture may also benefit the writer as although this exercise is a dying art, it allows us to reflect on life - and practise our handwriting! Writing on paper encourages a more considered approach when planning what we want to say, since we are unable to conveniently delete it as we are accustomed to doing on a laptop.

A letter is also a physical record of time and is something to be treasured. I have many letters received from loved ones before the days of emails, texts and messaging - these penned snapshots of life are now becoming increasingly rare.

So, take time to write that letter and pop it in the post for someone special. Imagine their surprise when they receive it in the 'snail mail'.

You may even receive one back!

MOOD BOOST 9

Go outside!

Mother nature may find it tricky to compete with the comfort of being indoors in January, but spending time under the big sky is beneficial.

In our modern world of screens and other stimuli contributing to mental fatigue, getting outside provides a sense of freedom. It increases physical activity, helps to reduce anxiety and fosters a feeling of being connected with nature. It also takes us away from indoor pollutants and supports our circadian rhythm for a good night's sleep.

On a dry day don't slump on the sofa, wrap up and enjoy a cuppa in the garden. Breathe in the fresh air, notice the flora and fauna around you and listen to the birds sing. Get active by taking a long walk or do some gardening to make you feel energised, grounded and focused.

Light up the outdoor firepit and invite loved ones to sit around it to chat and toast marshmallows while snuggled up under thick blankets. Go a step further and dust off the barbecue to cook a spicy meal outdoors, with a jug of hot mulled cider to share!

You will feel warm from head to toe!

MOOD BOOST 10

Take a nap!

Naps aren't just for babies; they can benefit adults too! January means less daylight hours which can make us feel tired. Taking 'forty winks' is an effective way to naturally increase energy levels and boost mood.

Investing in an afternoon snooze can improve alertness, enhance memory and allow the mind to clarify information taken in earlier in the day. Even if you are just lying down, the physical relaxation will benefit your immunity and creativity as well as reduce stress levels.

Don't feel guilty about taking a power nap - put your feet up and drift away! Napping longer than thirty minutes may cause you to suffer from sleep inertia, so be sure to set an alarm to avoid any grogginess and get the very best from your rest.

Sweet mini dreams!

MOOD BOOST 11

Feed the birds!

It is easy to take birds for granted as they are all around us, nesting in trees, swooping and soaring overhead, perching on rooftops and chirping in hedgerows.

Take some time out to observe their antics close up by placing a bird feeder by your window to encourage them to visit. They have their own schedules and squabbles just like us, which is amusing to watch.

Birds are facing so many challenges with many millions of birds lost in Britain over the past fifty years. Every January, the Royal Society for the Protection of Birds (RSPB) asks residents to take part in their annual Big Garden Birdwatch, which gives a valuable insight into how well British garden birds are faring.

It doesn't matter if you are a novice or know a lot about birds, you don't even need a garden to take part. See the RSPB website for details.

MOOD BOOST 12

Cuddle!

It is good to cuddle.

The human instinct to seek out physical connection with others is strong and has benefits for both the giver and receiver in many ways.

When we cuddle, our body releases less of the stress hormone cortisol and instead releases oxytocin, which helps to deal with stress and pain more effectively and supports the immune system.

Regular cuddling also enhances bonding and empathy as it communicates trust without speaking. This enables us to feel calmer which improves sleep, aids digestion and increases confidence levels.

Take time to hug your loved ones and fill your cuddle tank! If you don't have anyone close by then get a snuggle buddy. Body pillows and large soft toys can provide reassurance. Alternatively, invest in a weighted blanket which delivers the sensation of security and helps to soothe the nervous system - similar to how a baby feels when swaddled.

MOOD BOOST 13

Change your perspective!

It is amazing how a change of perspective can affect our mood. If we feel we are having a bad day or generally losing at life, it is helpful to step back and view it from another angle.

One method is to stand in front of a mirror and take a good look at yourself and the fascinating fusion of features inherited from your ancestors. Imagine them standing behind you, looking back at you in the mirror and feel their support for you.

Think about the sacrifice and hardship they have been through, which has resulted in you standing where you are today. Ask yourself what they would think about your life opportunities which they never had. Value yourself and your history and make your ancestors proud!

Another approach is to change your expectations of life. Rather than feeling frustrated about what you don't have, remind yourself of all the things you do, including the roof over your head, a wardrobe full of clothes and a warm meal. Appreciate how daily tasks, such as being able to go to work and clean the home, should not be taken for granted.

MOOD BOOST 14

Buy a lottery ticket!

We have to be in it to win it but even if we don't win it, imagining what we would do if we did, is beneficial for wellbeing!

Buying a lottery ticket stimulates the brain's reward - anticipation pathway. The realisation that purchasing a ticket offers a small possibility of hitting the jackpot can bring a lift to our day.

Taking a little time to dream about how it would feel to win and all the ways the money could be spent or shared with others, is a creative and positive exercise which generates optimism.

It is my belief that if you are meant to win, you will.

One ticket is all you need!

MOOD BOOST 15

Sing!

Whether or not we can carry a tune, singing is good for the soul. Evidence has shown that raising our voice in song releases feel good hormones and makes us feel great.

Singing in comfortable circumstances has been revealed to boost mood as it provides an acceptable way to express emotions, which can help us cope with stressful times. It also increases self-esteem and motivation, which has positive consequences in other areas of life.

Singing is an aerobic activity which stimulates the immune system, improves lung function and even increases our pain threshold. It is a mindful activity - as the focus on breathing, rhythm and tone halts negative thoughts and keeps us in the present.

Singing with others develops a sense of connection and inclusion, so consider joining a local choir or just enjoy performing for yourself.

Sing your heart out!

MOOD BOOST 16

Spend time with your pet!

There is nothing like hanging out with our pets to give spirits a lift. Whether we have a dog, cat, horse or hamster, their companionship gives purpose to our days and makes us smile.

Something as simple as watching our pet going about its daily routine has been shown to release feel good hormones, lower blood pressure and reduce stress levels. Research shows that just five minutes cuddling can release calming hormones for both the pet and the owner!

Give your pets the attention they deserve and boost your own mood at the same time. It doesn't matter whether you are exercising them, playing their favourite game, feeding them delicious treats or just relaxing in their company - they will love you for it.

If you don't have a pet, consider getting one but ensure you research which type would be the best fit for you and your lifestyle.

Dogs come in all shapes, sizes and temperaments. They can be a lot of fun as well as provide opportunities to meet new people during walks and training classes, but they are a big commitment. Cats are more independent and are great at reducing stress levels when purring on your lap. Smaller pets, such as hamsters, are less demanding.

If you can't dedicate yourself full time then try pet sitting for a neighbour who is out at work all day, or volunteer at an animal rescue centre - you get plenty of benefits but none of the expense.

MOOD BOOST 17

Bake!

Baking has a lot of potential to boost our mood and not just because of the tasty treat at the end. It can evoke wonderful memories from childhood and encourages us to live in the moment.

Methodically working through a recipe can bring comfort. The process of preparing and measuring and the rhythm of mixing and kneading is a grounding experience. Baking can enhance self-esteem, as well as provide a sense of connection and a chance to develop new skills.

Set aside some time to get creative in the kitchen. The recipe can be as simple or as complex as you like, the main thing is to have fun. Whether you make rich chocolate brownies, crisp cheese straws, yummy carrot cake or delectable custard tarts - infuse your home with delicious aromas and relish the mouthwatering results.

Take your home baked goodies into work to share at coffee break or box up your treats for friends and good neighbours to show you care. Create something indulgent for your partner to demonstrate your love.

MOOD BOOST 18

Get handy!

Did you know that using our hands is good for wellbeing?

Doing something physical with our hands can enhance brain function, create a sense of satisfaction and boost mood. This is due to a significant number of brain neurons being linked to hand movement.

Mundane chores which keep our hands busy but require little concentration, such as washing, kneading, polishing and scrubbing, can offer a welcome break from digital fatigue and help us to relax.

Specific tasks which result in something we can touch, e.g. carpentry or knitting, increase feel-good hormones and improve our attention span. Learning a new hands-on skill can nurture resilience and self-awareness, improve confidence and provide us with a feeling of joy.

So, brighten your day by doing some gardening or painting and don't moan about the washing up when you know it's good for you!

MOOD BOOST 19

List your accomplishments!

The power of the written word is strong. Research has shown that regularly recognising and writing down our accomplishments can reduce stress levels and increase self-confidence.

Listing our achievements allows the brain to identify our strengths and celebrate them. Taking time to remember past triumphs provides us with a sense of satisfaction and subconsciously instills us with the motivation and self-assurance to accomplish more in the future.

Whenever you complete a task that you feel proud of, add it to your list while it is fresh in your mind. Read your list when you need to boost your mood and appreciate how far you have come in life.

MOOD BOOST 20

Wish upon a star!

Long dark evenings provide plenty of opportunity to do a little stargazing. Although the night sky may appear endless, the stars offer us an anchor point and remind us how small we are. It is a perfect time to contemplate life and gain some perspective.

On a clear evening, wrap up in plenty of layers, grab a cushion and hot drink and head outside to your balcony, patio or front door step. Then spend a while observing the immense sky at night.

Take time to become familiar with the naked eye before investing in instruments to stargaze in more detail. Light and portable binoculars are great for observing the moon and meteor showers. Phone apps have the ability to identify all things celestial. If you fancy exploring deep sky objects, such as nebulae and star clusters, invest in a telescope.

Feel the wonder as you study the constellations and spot a shooting star or two. Be sure to make a wish - it may come true!

MOOD BOOST 21

Tackle your inbox!

Emails can quickly mount up and we may regularly feel swamped by the sheer amount we receive, especially with spam emails flooding our inbox, day after day after day. It is often tempting to ignore them or decide to deal with them later until the task seems insurmountable.

Use January to gain control of your 'email situation' once and for all. The process can be cathartic and you will finally be free from that nagging feeling every time you open your laptop.

Begin by responding to any emails that cannot wait, drop those you need to keep for future reference in appropriate files, unsubscribe from junk emails and then delete, delete, delete. Make a deal with yourself to do this once a day as doing so will prevent future email chaos - then obviously reward yourself with a treat!

MOOD BOOST 22
Pop some colour!

January may mean grey clouds and stark landscapes but our wardrobe does not have to follow suit. Bright and colourful shouldn't be kept for summer days as it is needed more than ever at this time of year, so make the effort to find some cheerful outfits that spark joy.

Even a neutral style can be enhanced by investing in a few vibrant items. Choosing a vivid coat, boots, scarf, gloves, belt, earrings, hat, lipstick or nail polish can make a positive and fun impact.

Different colours affect mood in different ways. Most of us know that warm tones stimulate the emotions and cool ones calm them, but the way we respond is also subjective. A bright neon blue tone can have a very different effect on the subconscious mind than a muted or pale shade of blue. Some may evoke good memories and others, not.

Select your preference on what suits you and makes you feel good, then create a unique collection. It may also inspire those around you!

MOOD BOOST 23
Make plans!

Studies have shown that the pleasure obtained from having good experiences outweighs those received from material purchases.

Organising a trip away is valuable for our mental wellbeing as it provides a significant mood boost. The anticipation of an exciting event in the future can produce a substantial increase in happy hormones - apparently almost as many as the event itself!

January is perfect to start planning a few dates in the diary with your favourite people. This is a great time of year to make the most of any last-minute holiday deals and weekend break offers, or simply take a day trip somewhere new. Even arranging a simple lunch with friends will make you feel lifted and give you something to look forward to.

Book that date in the diary!

MOOD BOOST 24
Dance!

When we hear a good piece of music, it is hard to keep still. Dance seems to be part of our psyche with evidence going back thousands of years, and it is no wonder as it can be transformative. We jiggle and sway to the beat from an early age, as many a baby video will prove, and we keep our feet tapping well into our later years.

Dance is accessible to everyone and enables us to feel care free and live in the moment. The joyful movement stimulates a body and mind connection and provides a dopamine high which makes us feel great.

It also raises our heart rate, gets our blood pumping, increases mental and physical agility, enhances spatial awareness and improves creativity.

Play your favourite tunes out loud and groove to your heart's content.

MOOD BOOST 25

Buy yourself flowers!

It's amazing how flowers can boost our mood and give our home a cheery vibe during dreary January weather. We all deserve a bunch or two of radiant blooms to warm and brighten the grey winter days.

Treat yourself to some beautiful bouquets and place them in vases around the house where there is a plenty of footfall - such as the living room and the hall. You will feel an instant lift whenever you see them.

If cut flowers are not really your thing then a potted plant is a great alternative as it brings the outside, inside! Cyclamen, poinsettias and orchids provide a welcome splash of colour and the aloe vera plant, peace lily and spider plant are effective at purifying the air. English ivy can be useful for removing airborne mould during damp weather.

If you fancy a green-thumb project, start from scratch by planting a selection of bulbs into vibrant pots and place on a window sill. Marvel at how amazing nature is as they sprout and flourish into mini miracles.

MOOD BOOST 26

Make a fund pot!

A fund pot is a great incentive to stop spending hard earned money on wasteful purchases or unhealthy habits and save the cash for something much more valuable, useful or exciting instead.

Every time you would normally spend cash on items you don't need, or vices that you would love to quit, put the money you would have spent into a pot and place it out of easy reach. If you don't handle cash often, set up a separate 'fund pot file' in your online bank account.

Boost your mood by watching your savings grow and think about how you will spend it. Anticipate tempting treats such as a meal out or a new pair of shoes. Maybe you want to save for a holiday of a lifetime or surprise a loved one with an extra special gift. Alternatively, enjoy building up a proper rainy-day fund to give you peace of mind.

MOOD BOOST 27

Phone a friend!

It's good to talk. Research suggests that verbal interactions with those you trust can boost mood. Phoning a friend for a catch up increases our sense of belonging, reduces stress and encourages optimism.

Many of us have busy lives and it is sometimes tempting to send a quick and convenient text to stay in touch, but these messages can be misinterpreted and lack a human connection. Scheduling time to actually talk to friends and family nurtures the relationship, and doing it on a regular basis can support our mental health.

Research suggests that speaking on the phone can provide a richer, more intimate experience than a video call, as attention is focused only on the voice. Tuning into the pitch and tone, familiar expressions and unique linguistic cues helps to form a stronger, more powerful bond.

Don't delay - make that call today!

MOOD BOOST 28
Act like a child!

We all love a little nostalgia from our childhood but it turns out that it can actually boost our wellbeing. Being an adult comes with a lot of responsibilities but taking time out to channel our inner child can support a young mental attitude and make us feel happier.

Stop doing the chores, put paying the bills on hold and recapture that magical feeling of youth by doing things you enjoyed as a little person.

Take a trip down memory lane as you ride a bike and feel the wind in your hair. Listen to the old chart hits you loved and transport your mind back to your first school disco. Watch classic cartoons from your past which had you racing to the TV in case you missed them.

Look in the attic for your old toys and reread a beloved bedtime story book. Go for a walk and splash in the puddles or buy a hula hoop and get those hips swinging. Play hide and seek and hopscotch, or reload a video game from your past and see if you still have the skills to win.

Meet up with childhood friends and visit places you used to hang out together. Eat retro snacks and have a good giggle as you look through your old photograph albums - and wonder where the years went!

MOOD BOOST 29

Meditate!

Meditating improves mood as the technique trains our mind to redirect thought patterns and behaviour. Regular meditation can reduce anxiety, increase clarity, improve sleep and also enhance cognitive skills and emotional health. There are various types of meditation but the following version is quite simple and accessible.

Find a quiet, comfortable place and sit in a relaxed but upright position. Close your eyes and take some slow and deep breaths from your belly.

Become aware of how your body feels - notice any discomfort, warmth or coolness. Then focus all of your attention on your breath going in and out. When your mind begins to wander, acknowledge it and then gently bring it back to focus on your breathing.

Do this as many times as you need. Your mind will inevitably roam and you may daydream as this is normal. Don't judge yourself for it, just focus back on your breathing. When you feel ready, open your eyes and you're done. The more you meditate, the more you will improve your ability to bring your mind back to the present and benefit from it.

MOOD BOOST 30
Make a bucket list!

Ever wanted to go skydiving, speak another language, move abroad, feed a sloth or see Niagara Falls? Whatever it is that floats our boat, we shouldn't let it drift away. A bucket list is a great way to clarify our desires about the things we want to achieve in life before our time is up!

Write down all the things you want to do in the near or distant future, then pin it somewhere where you can see it regularly. This will not only give you a boost but will also subconsciously encourage you to take those steps needed towards realising your dreams.

Include some smaller ambitions as well as the big stuff. This could be anything from seeing a favourite musical, improving your personal best, being able to juggle, do a handstand or make the perfect souffle.

Don't limit your imagination - be bold and determined!

MOOD BOOST 31

Indulge yourself!

A little of what we fancy does us good!

Studies have revealed that when we allow ourselves a treat, our self-esteem increases and we feel content. This act of self-care is supportive to our wellbeing because it encourages us to maintain healthy habits and prevents us becoming resentful - which can affect those around us.

Reward yourself after a tedious task by preparing something delicious to eat. Cheer yourself up on a rainy day by relaxing on the sofa with your favourite hot drink. Indulge yourself after a particularly stressful event by purchasing a little luxury gift which is just for you!

Remember, the definition of a treat is an event or item that gives you pleasure and is *out of the ordinary*. Too many extravagances may lead to feelings of being out of control and guilt, or excessive spending.

Save your indulgences for times when you really need them, then enjoy!

CONCLUSION

So, there you are! A collection of ideas, advice, entertainment and activities that have truly enhanced my January days and I am so pleased to have shared them with you.

I hope you have enjoyed reading my book and discovered a few gems to inspire you and make January a time to look forward to. Communicate this positive vibe with your loved ones and encourage them to approach January with a sense of optimism.

Remember, life is rarely perfect but we can make the best of the time we have. January marks the beginning of a new year and with a little hope and intention, it can become a month of real opportunity to lay down strong foundations for the future.

Take it a day at a time. Plan a little, relax a lot and have fun finding your January Joy!

ABOUT THE AUTHOR

Sophie Hayward lives with her family in Cornwall and enjoys nothing more than long coastal walks which end in a cosy pub.

She holds BSc (Hons) degrees in Psychology and Marketing and is an advocate of hygge - inspired by the culture of her Danish mother.

This, combined with her love of winter, has provided the inspiration for her first book, January Joy.

Printed in Great Britain
by Amazon

a864d7a3-b595-4cdb-9299-3b6d59962d35R01